REFLECTIONS

ON

SPIRITUAL AWAKENING

Insights from the
Asbury Awakening
& Beyond

BILL ELLIFF

Reflections on Spiritual Awakening: Insights from the Asbury Awakening and Beyond
By Bill Elliff

Published by TruthINK Publications
6600 Crystal Hill Road
North Little Rock, Arkansas 72118

Cover Design | Dave Lewis

ISBN: 978-0-9831168-8-2

Printed in the United States of America

CONTENTS

AS YOU BEGIN ...

Spiritual awakenings are a part of the regular ways of God. Throughout history, God has brought needed course corrections to His people. Without moments and seasons of God's outpourings—both personally and corporately—the church would be adrift because of the weakness of our flesh, the incessant pressure of the world, and the devious activity of our ever-present Enemy. We know this is true, not only because of the Biblical record but also by even a cursory look at our own lives. "Prone to wander, Lord, I feel it; prone to leave the God I love," the songwriter lamented.

In His vast mercy, God oversees His Bride and chooses to rend the heavens and make Himself known in seasons of revival and awakening with Divine precision. He does this in our lives, our churches, and our nations. These visitations are glorious and extraordinary, reviving His people and accelerating His work among the unconverted. The United States has been blessed to have seen five such nationwide course corrections every 50 or so years since the early 1700s. Each time they have been desperately needed.

Asbury University is a college soaked in revival history and the scene of multiple such movements. It is located 55 miles from Cane Ridge, Kentucky, the scene of one of the great outpourings in the Second Great Awakening in 1801. Barton Stone, the Presbyterian pastor of Cane Ridge, wrote of an extraordinary moment that occurred in a three-day scheduled "sacrament" meeting. Normally it would be attended by a few hundred people. God chose to manifest Himself.

> The roads were literally crowded with wagons, car-riages, horsemen, and footmen, moving to the solemn camp. The sight was affecting. It was judged, by mil-itary men on the ground, that there were between twenty and thirty thousand collected. Four or five preachers were frequently speaking at the same time, in different parts of the encampment, without confu-sion. The Methodist and Baptist preachers aided in the work, and all appeared cordially united in it—of one mind and one soul, and the salvation of sinners seemed to be the great object of all. We all engaged in singing the same songs of praise—all united in prayer—all preached the same things—free salvation urged upon all by faith and repentance.

> A particular description of this meeting would fill a large volume, and then the half would not be told. The numbers converted will be known only in eternity. Many things transpired there, which were so much like miracles, that if they were not, they had the same ef-fects as miracles on infidels and unbelievers; for many of them by these were convinced that Jesus was the Christ, and bowed in submission to him. This meeting continued six or seven days and nights, and would have continued longer, but provisions for such a mul-titude failed in the neighborhood. To this meeting many had come from Ohio and other distant parts,

who returned home and diffused the same spirit in
their neighborhoods, and the same works followed.[1]

The theology, spirit, and history of Asbury, a Wesleyan Holiness
school, has led to multiple seasons of revival, beginning with a
dorm room prayer meeting that extended for days with E. Stanley
Jones in 1905.

On February 8, 2023, God chose to visit Asbury again with an
unusual spiritual movement. Tens of thousands of hungry people descended on this small community of 6,000 from all over
the world in sixteen days to witness and experience this spiritual
outpouring. It has continued to spread to other campuses and
churches, and only time will tell if it is a lasting or temporary season. But even if it does not continue with the same intensity, the
church has been awakened in great measure to the greatness and
mercy of God, for which all of us should be grateful.

My wife and I were privileged to participate in these wonderful
days in Hughes Chapel for five days on two occasions. I found
myself waking up each night and recording what I observed and
praying for the spread of this precious outpouring across the nation
and the world. These are some brief reflections from these days,
recorded in real time, and offered as a humble attempt to help
others embrace the reality of what God has done and stimulate an
increased cry for more.

Bill Elliff
Little Rock, Arkansas
March 28, 2023

---

[1] *Voices from Cane Ridge*, edited by Rhodes Thompson, Bethany Press, St. Louis,
MO, 1954, Pg 31-134

CHAPTER 1

THE BEGINNING

FEBRUARY 11, 2023

YESTERDAY MY WIFE, Holly, and I decided to make the nine-hour drive from our home to Wilmore, Kentucky to observe and experience what God seems to be doing, once again, at Asbury University. I'm so grateful we did.

FEBRUARY 1970

... was the year God broke into a normal chapel service which continued non-stop for the next seven days and nights at Asbury University. The Jesus Movement was already beginning, but the Asbury Revival accelerated it dramatically. Eventually, teams of students left Asbury and went across the country to 130 college campuses, telling the story. Everywhere they went, revival and awakening broke out. We came this week because our lives were transformed by the movement at Asbury in 1970 and the Jesus movement that occurred. We have longed for and sought revival ever since.

FEBRUARY 2023

This past Wednesday morning (February 8), the Lord moved in another chapel service in Hughes Auditorium. That single service has continued morning and night and is now on its fourth day (Saturday, February 11). I talked to one of the leaders who was there on Wednesday. His observation was that these last days have been days of consecration, but we are yet to see what could happen in the days ahead.

I hesitate to even write of this because I've only been here one day. I have no idea of the magnitude of what God has done in the last few days.

Many are asking me what I'm observing, though, so I would give these cursory thoughts. Heaven records the full reality.

1. This is real. God is very present.

2. Several hundred gathered in the morning hours, but the crowd filled every seat by the afternoon in the 1500-seat auditorium.

3. Since Wilmore is almost exclusively a college town with very little else, the crowd is primarily students, although many, like myself, are coming in to see what God is doing.

4. Students from many other colleges are here, having traveled from across the country. The leaders at Asbury are very aware of this, even commissioning them at one point today to go back and cry out for revival on their campus.

5. Worship is glorious, unified, and simple. A piano and guitar, led by various student teams who understand that worship is not performance.

6. The altar is almost always full. Wonderful prayer counselors from Asbury are helping them.

7. There are wise leaders from the University who are helping shepherd the moment. I'm sure they have learned from the past movements how to steward this best.

8. It is not weird. Everything is extremely orderly but vibrant, spontaneous, and powerful.

9. In some ways, it is a worship-based, Spirit-led, Scripture-fed prayer gathering (to copy Daniel Henderson's term). It is just what we should be doing all the time: waiting before God, worshiping Him, praying to Him, listening to Him, responding to Him, and being shepherded by wise leaders who see themselves merely as facilitators of God's activity. (The Holy Spirit is a very good leader, by the way. Far better than mere men.)

10. When the microphones were opened for testimonies, there were long lines of grateful people telling what God has done in the last 72 hours. Healing—both emotional, spiritual, and physical has happened in glorious ways. Very real and profound things are occurring quickly in hundreds of lives.

11. Within the first hour, I had moved from a spectator to a humble participant.

12. The unity and worship are heavenly. No pretense, pride, or show. No manipulation. You don't want to leave.

13. The Scripture was read this afternoon for a long time by multiple people, washing over the congregation. After each Scripture, the response was, "The Word of God, and we believe it!"

14. People seem to be moved by Christ deeply, not merely by emotion, although emotions are present. (How could we not be emotional if God is in the room in power and lives are being transformed?)

Samuel Davies, the president of Princeton who was in the First Great Awakening, said that during that time, "the gospel became almighty and carried everything before it." In that nationwide movement, 15% of the population of America came to faith in Christ. Whole towns reported that there were no adults left who were unconverted.

Asbury is not that yet, but it is a beautiful mercy drop. In these days of social media and rapid communication, the flame could spread quickly. Millions of desperate believers in our nation are crying out for the next nationwide spiritual awakening. Small outbreaks are happening everywhere.

Asbury has a history of such movements, even before 1970. Their expectant faith has provided fertile ground for the Lord's visitation. (Faith is undoubtedly an ingredient in why this is happening. There were some places where Jesus could do nothing because of their unbelief).

AND NOW ...

Pray for Asbury ... and pray for your church and the churches and people of your city. Cry out as never before, pleading with our reviving God to be merciful to us. Seek revival personally and fervently. Ask God to search your heart and remove anything that is quenching the flow of His Spirit. Ask God to break through your church this Sunday with a Wind that will not stop.

Pray that God would send revival to His church and then a mighty awakening to the lost. Ask Him to manifest Himself in power so that millions can be brought to Christ and the church can rise again into its missionary calling. Pray for the acceleration and rapid expansion of the gospel ... for His Kingdom to come.

As I spoke to the hotel receptionist this morning, she told me they were sold out of rooms. "We were not prepared for revival," she said.

May it not be true of us.

CHAPTER 2

THE QUIET ORDER

FEBRUARY 13, 2023

THE QUIET, PRECIOUS movement of God continues into its sixth day in Wilmore, Kentucky, on the campus of Asbury University. This is not the first time an extended movement has occurred here. Similar movements happened in 1905 when a prayer meeting led by E. Stanly Jones lasted for many days. In the '50s, two other outpourings occurred, and in 1970, a chapel service extended for seven days and nights. God used it as a catalyst to fuel the nationwide awakening that was ultimately labeled the "Jesus Movement."

I've had the privilege of sitting in Hughes Auditorium, where this is happening for the last two days, watching and experiencing this extraordinary movement. Only for the purposes of explanation (and no other reason), I would mention that I have been a pastor for 54 years serving in the Baptist stream. Revival touched down on our small Arkansas school in 1970 (Ouachita Baptist University). My wife and I witnessed firsthand the manifest presence of God as a noonday chapel went throughout the day, canceling classes and changing lives. We've never been the same.

I've been a student of God's revival movements across history for over fifty years. I traveled for several years to churches, helping them pursue God in revival. I was a founding member of the OneCry initiative that seeks to help pastors and churches pursue God for revival and spiritual awakening. I have spoken and written a great deal about this theme, for it is the desperate need of our day. Our deteriorating culture illustrates that it is time for a needed movement from Heaven. Samuel Davies of the First Great Awakening said, "There are eras when only a large outpouring of the Spirit can produce a public general reformation."

We have seen seasons of His movement in the church I helped plant 25 years ago. One particular season happened in 2011 after six months of fasting and praying by the congregation. One Sunday morning, the Lord interrupted our normal schedule with an unusual outpouring of His Spirit which lasted through the afternoon. That continued—every night except Saturdays—for three to four hours each evening for five weeks. It was not weird, nor wildly uncomfortable, but the quiet movement of the Spirit, filled with prayer, repentance, salvation, and spontaneous baptisms by new believers. Many came to faith in Christ.

I mention these things for one reason alone (please understand). It is certainly not to boast but to explain who is writing this article to help those who would criticize this movement from a distance.

THE QUIET ORDER OF ASBURY

Last night, I saw some self-appointed critics of the Asbury movement on social media. Of course, they had not been to Hughes Auditorium but had just "heard" that this and that was happening. When I read their second and third-hand reports, I was shocked, but not surprised. God always has his critics.

What is happening at Asbury (as I have witnessed first-hand) has some beautiful, biblical components. This is what I've observed.

VIBRANT, POWERFUL WORSHIP.

Worship is being led by various student teams. Some are more proficient than others, but all are humble. We do not know their names.[2]

There are no fog machines nor dramatic lighting—just piano and guitar by unnamed students worshiping God. We are singing songs that would be familiar to most of us, often just acapella, with no instruments. Contemporary songs are sung, often interspersed by the hymns of the church. There are no words on the screen, and they do not seem to be needed.

INTENSE AND INTENTIONAL HUMILITY

The wise pastors on Asbury's staff who are gently shepherding this movement keep reminding us that there are no superstars and that no one is to be exalted except Jesus. They have encouraged us to get lower and lower and lower under Him, exalting Him higher and higher. I have personally watched them stop a person or two who may have tried to hijack the meeting. They realize that God's manifest presence is precious and desperately needed. They want no one or no thing to quench or grieve His Spirit.

---

[2] *I discovered later that each team that was chosen to lead was taken to a makeshift "Consecration Room," often for over an hour, to prepare their hearts to lead.*

LIFE-CHANGING TESTIMONIES

The leaders, at times, will open the microphones for a season of testimonies of what God has done. They instruct the crowd to observe these ABC's:

- All glory to God alone

- Brief

- Current

They stand with microphone in hand and wisely shepherd these moments. They will close the lines when they sense it's time to move forward.

Often during these testimonies, when they sense God repeating a theme, they have paused and called for those with the same issues to stand, and for people to gather around them and pray.

GUIDED PRAYER

At various times, they have led us into corporate prayer. Instructions are given, and then we've turned in small groups and cried out to God.

At the altar, they have a continuous team of prayer counselors, identified by lanyards around their necks, who are helping those in need and praying with them. They have gently invited the people to come to these trained counselors for prayer.

UNASHAMED WITNESS

Everywhere, people are sharing with others in need outside the auditorium. God is opening people's lips and giving them the Acts

4 courage to "speak the word of God with boldness." The result is what you would expect—the gospel is spreading rapidly, and many are coming to faith in Christ.

SPIRITUAL, EMOTIONAL, AND EVEN PHYSICAL HEALING

Many are giving testimony of how God is instantly releasing them from years of bondage to addictions. Release from past hurts, bitterness, fear, is happening quickly for the humble ones who admit their need and cry to the Savior. Some are testifying of physical healings, just as occurred in the Book of Acts, but this is not at all the dominant theme of the meetings. The theme is Jesus—exalting Him, surrendering to Him, and testifying of Him to others.

PREACHING

One prognosticator on social media proclaimed that this was not of God because there was no preaching. I smiled, because there have been moments of preaching throughout and a "regular" sermon every single night, delivered humbly by godly pastors.

WISE LEADERSHIP

I cannot say enough about this. I have been in many moments of intense revival. I have led in a number of these moments. I stood at a microphone for five weeks, shepherding a movement of God for 3-4 hours a night.

I'm overwhelmed by the wise, quiet, strong, loving leadership of those in charge. It is not dominating and not restrictive. They are discerning God's movement and cooperating. They are giving instruction and direction when needed.

CONSISTENCY WITH THE WAYS OF GOD

The Jesus movement was characterized by vibrant, simple worship and constant witness to the gospel. I was there. The church, by and large, reacted to the "hippies" who were being saved and the more current expressions of worship. Many churches ridiculed this and quenched the Spirit, unwilling to accept new wineskins. Most of these churches have plateaued and died. The churches that humbly opened the door to lost people and wisely shepherded God's activity, exploded. Calvary Chapel, a small California church, kept responding to God and, in the Jesus movement's wake, started 1400 churches.

Two things characterized the 1857 revival: First, fervent noon-day prayer meetings that grew from six people (with Jeremiah Lanphier) to 50,000 people every day in New York City alone. And secondly, unashamed testimony and witnessing. There were simple "rules" that they used to guide the prayer meetings. They lasted precisely one hour, beginning at noon each day. It spread across the country. Prayer requests came from around the world. I've read many of those actual requests—most are for the salvation of someone somebody loved. In revival, our hearts return to beat with the heart of God, whose great desire is for people of every tongue, tribe, and nation to come to Him.

When the church begins to pray, that IS revival, for we are usually prayerless. When that reviving turns to fervent, unashamed witnessing and the rapid acceleration of the gospel, we term that "spiritual awakening," for that is exactly what God is doing among the lost.

GIVING GOD TIME AND WAITING

The revival here is not hurried or rushed. There are long periods of stillness and waiting. If you want to rush in, get a big dose of God and rush out, don't come. God works on His timetable. We give God little time and almost no silence. What is happening here is occurring because thirsty people are waiting before God. In time, He speaks to one, then another, bringing them back to intimacy with Him. I've always thought that we don't experience God because we put Him on our timetable. Waiting is a lost art. It is turning our full attention to Him until He makes Himself known.

SPREADING

As of the fifth day of the movement, 22 colleges have sent groups of students here, hoping to see the same outbreak on their campuses. It would not surprise me if that was how this exploded nationwide, for students are most tender and willing. It is also no coincidence that a very carefully-made movie about the Jesus Revolution is coming out by our friend, Jon Erwin, February 24 and that the Collegiate National Day of Prayer broadcast has been scheduled for over a year to be broadcast from Asbury on February 23. We should pray that these will further accelerate God's work.

OVERWHELMING LOVE

One of the leaders spoke to us last night about the beginning of the revival when a pastor spoke of hypocritical, self-seeking love. He remarked that what these days have done has reversed that. Asbury has become a sanctuary of the love of God. That is the essence of God (He IS love) and has been the hallmark of every moment when He is placed again on His rightful throne in our hearts, homes, and churches. "Heaven a World of Love" was preached by Jonathan Edwards. And revival is heaven coming down.

SO WHAT IS YOUR RESPONSE?

I talked with a friend who reminded me of this beautiful truth from a missionary involved in the great revival in Shantung, China, in the late 20s.

> "We heard of the revival in Korea, which began in 1907. It was a mighty movement and had been born through a prayer-revival among missionaries. Oh, to be able to go there and bring back some glowing coals to our own field! But the journey was long and expensive and I had not the money. As I prayed for money and looked for an answer, a definite word was sent instead: "What you want through that journey you may be given here, where you are, in answer to prayer." The words were a tremendous challenge. I gave my solemn promise: 'Then I will pray until I receive. Having pledged myself ... the first conscious thought was: Then prayer means as much as that, and that my promise should be kept means as much as that.' That experience helped me to endure through the almost twenty years which were to pass before the first small beginnings of revival were visible. Truly, God

works unhurriedly." (Marie Monsen, missionary nurse
to north China, describing how she came to pray for
the revival that burned there from 1927-1932)

You don't have to come to Kentucky to experience revival and awakening. "The kingdom of God is here," Jesus said, and He has gladly chosen to give us the Kingdom.

AND FINALLY ...

Coming out of Hughes auditorium, with its love and grace and humility, and reading the words of some critics on social media was revealing. The pride of their words was apparent when seen against the backdrop of the presence of God. The spirit of such judgments came through the page and was glaring in its self-righteousness. It's wise to examine things carefully, but foolish to make swift judgments without close examination and real knowledge.

If you are tempted to criticize this movement flippantly, it might be wise to heed the counsel of Gamaliel when his religious colleagues criticized the early disciples.

> "So in the present case, I say to you, stay away from these men
> and let them alone, for if this plan or action is of men, it will be
> overthrown; but if it is of God, you will not be able to overthrow
> them; or else you may even be found fighting against God."
> (Acts 5:38-39)

CHAPTER 3

SHEPHERDING IN THE MIDST OF GOD'S MOVEMENTS

FEBRUARY 14, 2023

A RADIO HOST asked me today how I would describe revival. I answered with what I heard Richard Owen Roberts say once. "I can answer that in one word: God." The history of revival is one long story of God. God's mercy. God's gracious intervention and initiation. It is God bringing His people to desperation. It is God initiating unceasing prayer. It is God letting us see the evil that comes when we don't walk with Him as a church. It is God, in great graciousness, opening the windows of heaven to wash and purify His church and set her back on mission. And then God awakening lost sinners and ushering them into His kingdom.

Richard Owen Roberts describes revival as "The extraordinary movement of the Spirit of God that produces extraordinary results." God is always moving, but in times of revival and awakening, the work of God is dramatically accelerated. First, reviving the church, then exploding in spiritual awakening among the lost.

In the First Great Awakening, 15% of the population came to faith. (If that happened in the Dallas/Ft.Worth area, it would be 1.2 million people. Nationally, it would be 50 million people.) In the

1857 revival, one million people came to faith out of a population of 30 million. Only God could do that. No program, no plan.

Reports are now coming in that multiple campuses across America are beginning to experience similar movements like Asbury (which has now filled all three auditoriums on the college and seminary campuses). We are also hearing reports of churches experiencing, last Sunday and this week, extraordinary stirrings of God's presence.

So, as pastors and spiritual leaders, what do we do? How do we shepherd in the midst of God's movements?

Please don't think that I am writing this as an expert. I have observed, firsthand at Asbury the last few days, the wise leadership of the Campus Pastor and others. In 2011, God broke into a normal service at our church. The service went for hours and then extended, completely unplanned, for five weeks, every night except Saturdays. I was involved as the pastor in leading with our other pastors.

What I observed happening at Asbury was almost identical to the mercy drop we experienced. Leading in those times can be confusing. None of us have ever been in a moment like (I believe) we are about to experience. So, this is merely a humble attempt to give some thoughts to us as leaders.

1. LET THE SPIRIT OF GOD LEAD HIS CHURCH

The Holy Spirit is a great leader! Perfect, in fact. But we rarely let Him be in charge. We plan the program and then work the plan. The results are insipid and often utterly contrary to what God desires.

Wise leaders in these days will know that they must lead with humility, prayerfully and carefully listening to the Spirit and following His promptings. During the 2011 revival in our church, I never knew what was going to happen 10 minutes later, but I always knew exactly what I was to do in the moment (that is not an exaggeration). Don't be afraid to let Him lead.

This requires that we are personally right with Him and listening to Him. You will be surprised how many on your team do not understand this or are ill-equipped to lead by God-initiation. If you are not right with God, go to the altar. Ask Him to cleanse you. Confess all known sins. Lay aside every doubtful habit. Clear your conscience with others and be filled with his Spirit.

But also, if God has placed you in leadership ... LEAD! Don't just look to others. The people need shepherds who will listen to Him and then lead the congregation humbly.

2. GUARD YOUR HEART

The quickest thing to stop revival is pride. Evan Roberts of the Welsh Revival (in which 100,000 people came to faith in nine months) was so afraid of this that he often would not enter a room where they were expecting Him. He was fearful that their attention would be on him and not God.

Seeing God move in power opens a broad gate to pride if we think it is something we've done. Revival is heady stuff. Just look at what happened BEFORE the revival and compare the difference between what we can do and what God does in power. God will not come where leaders are strutting. He knows He cannot entrust His activity to them.

At Asbury right now, the leaders model this beautifully, constantly calling everyone to understand that Jesus is the center of attention—no worship leader, personality, preacher, etc.

3. DON'T EXAGGERATE

Pastors are masters of exaggeration. Exaggeration is lying and is always done to make one look better. It will quench the Spirit (see Ananias in Acts 5). If eight people were saved, don't "round it up" to 10. State what God is doing very carefully. And give Him all the glory.

Don't try to make something happen by overstating what is happening. Let your words be few ... and accurate.

4. LET THE BODY SPEAK

The hallmark of many of God's great awakenings has been the unashamed testimonies of His people. When the room is pregnant with stories, open the microphone and let the people bless the Lord! Revival spreads this way. How can we glorify God if we do not hear what He is doing in real-time?

A practical thought is to instruct people about brevity and giving God all the glory. About sharing current stories, not past ones. And it is wise for pastors to shepherd the microphones, sense what God is saying, and follow that testimony with a Scriptural word or a call to prayer or response. *(Appendix 1 gives a practical guide for leading a time of testimony).*

Tell the story beyond the services. A blessed result of COVID may have been God's means to prepare us for this through the rise and use of the internet, television, radio, podcasts, and video.

The presence of our media resources means that this revival could spread worldwide quickly. The telegraph was invented right before the 1857 revival in America and aided its spread.

5. WORSHIP SIMPLY

We often feel that our best worship must be produced, carefully developed, and perfected. Most seasons of revival have been marked by spontaneous singing, often acapella. It can be off-key, stumbling over words, on your face, hands raised. God wants our hearts to be humbly focused on Him alone. For our praise to be pure. He loves the sound of His children worshiping Him, and the world is amazed at pure worship.

Help your people by providing the easiest ways to worship. Welcome a spontaneous song coming from the seats. Don't try to manage worship. Listen to the Lord and follow His promptings.

6. TARRY

One of the reasons we see little of God is that we do not give Him time. Asbury has been fueled by students who are willing to give God hours, even through the night. There is much in Scripture about waiting on God that we don't understand because we think everything depends on our fast-paced human work.

Wait on God. He comes to those who wait. Sing quietly, read His Word, and wait before Him in prayer. And in all things, put your attention on Him. Don't try to manipulate anything in a service, but if you sense God wants to extend the service, invite those who desire to stay to remain and keep going. People will make their choices.

The movement at Asbury started after a chapel service when the pastors invited those who wanted to meet with God to remain. Twenty students stayed. Later they were joined by hundreds and now by thousands. And we pray soon, by millions.

7. EMBRACE THE NEXT GENERATION

The church must be re-birthed and re-discovered by each generation. The wineskins may need to change. There's nothing sacred about a wineskin. Wineskins are designed to hold and release the wine, just as Jesus said.

At Asbury, they are holding the first rows open at all times for students. "We are a university," one of the leaders said, "And our passion is for these students under our watch to encounter God." That should be every pastor's passion. Let go of the past and your particular preferences. The Jesus Movement in the 70s was quenched prematurely (many believe) by pastors and church leaders who did not live for the next generation.

It looks like God has chosen, once again, to begin His best work among students who are willing to surrender fully, live unashamedly, and go anywhere and do anything for the sake of the gospel. God is raising up our next generation of pastors, missionaries, and spiritual leaders, and wise are the leaders who see this and give them room to lead and experience the manifest presence of God.

8. PRAY!

Revival is fueled by prayer. Pray without ceasing (that's not an impossibility, by the way, but should be the standard operating procedure for our lives and churches). Pray about everything. Prayer indicates we understand our pride and desperately need God in the equation.

Share about what God is doing in your churches and campus meetings this week. Call the people to cry out to God that He would not pass them by! Wait in His presence, worship Him, read His Word, open the altar for prayer, and don't look at the clock. It is your worst enemy. There is no clock in heaven.

9. PREPARE FOR SPIRITUAL WARFARE

You must understand the Enemy enough to know that he will explode in activity as revival accelerates. He is not pleased and has many powerful resources at his disposal. Watch out for Sanballat and Tobiah who will try to call you off the wall of God's great work. Recognize the Enemy's activity and stop it by God's authority. He has no legal right to one inch of God's church and movement. But he will try ... and try again.

We must be strong in the Lord, put on the full armor constantly, and pray at all times. As pastors, we must protect our flocks over whom we keep watch, guarding them from the wolves.

You might be very surprised who Satan will try to use. Some will oppose God's movement, and Satan will constantly be whispering in your ear to stop, to be distracted, or to slow down God's activity. Resist Him, firm in the faith, and he must flee. Don't let his temporary attacks divert you from the advance at hand.

10. PERSEVERE!

During our five-week experience of God's movement several years ago, one of our staff asked if we could restart some of the ancillary meetings. I reminded him that he might never see this happen again in his lifetime, and we would continue to meet in God's presence till He directed otherwise.

Revival is tiring, exhausting in fact, but refreshing at the same time. If you are a leader, there is a serious cost, a price to pay, as you give yourself to the many demands of a season of great harvest. You must be willing to persevere. Get rest when you can. Eat when you can, but remember that you are in a battlefield advance. Be encouraged by God's advice ...

> He who gathers in summer is a son who acts wisely, but
> he who sleeps in harvest is a son who acts shamefully.
> (Proverbs 10:5).

It's harvest time! We don't deserve it, but God does. He deserves a church returning to Him. A new generation rising up to follow Him. Millions of new believers giving Him the glory He deserves. A new missionary advance across the world. He deserves unceasing prayer and attention and full obedience.

He deserves revival and awakening.

CHAPTER 4

OVERCOMING FEAR

FEBRUARY 15, 2023

WHEN GOD CALLS us into new realms of spiritual experience, it can create great fear. Right now, we are seeing a revival movement at Asbury University and many other places that will take us where we have never been. Those who study the movements of God would tell you that it could explode across our nation—perhaps across our world.

What will you do? Many will criticize, which can often be nothing more than a convenient way to avoid addressing your life before God. Some will ignore God's movement. Some will go to a certain place and then stop because the cost may seem too high, the unknowns too uncertain.

Will you walk away in fear? Fear of the unknown? Fear of your inability? Fear of what might happen if you really let the Spirit of God lead your life and your church? Fear of the cost of revival? Fear that your preconceived ideas of convenient, Americanized Christianity will be disturbed?

IT'S NATURAL

Paul was afraid in the city of Corinth. The reason we know this is because Jesus doesn't waste words. He comes to him in Acts 18:9-10 with an encouragement that addresses his fear (and ours). He knew Paul needed an infusion of boldness.

> *And the Lord said to Paul in the night by a vision, "Do not be **afraid** any longer, but go on speaking and do not be silent; for I am with you, and no man will attack you in order to harm you, for I have many people in this city."*
> *(Acts 18:9-10)*

Paul knew that if he kept speaking and the spiritual movement kept spreading, he could be persecuted. It could become hard, uncomfortable, and challenging. There would be enemies and critics. It had happened before. At Corinth, he had worked among the religious Jews, finally "shaking the dust off his feet" and telling them he was going to the Gentiles because they would not listen. God directed Paul to move next door to the synagogue to a Gentile house which was repulsive to a self-righteous Jew.

Suddenly, the work of God was becoming multi-ethnic. God was asking Paul to go to a crowd that any self-respecting Jew would never consider. It was a perfect recipe for fear—an uncomfortable, new direction. And Paul was obviously afraid. This step was a new wineskin, a different paradigm from what had existed in the religious establishment.

In the Jesus Movement in the 1970s—the last nationwide movement of God we have seen that was sparked by an almost identical beginning at Asbury college—God began to work among students, and the somewhat rebellious group of people called "hippies." They began to come to Christ in record numbers all across America. When they began to go into the churches, (who were comfortable in their normal Christian routines), many churches rejected this out of fear. Those churches who recognized the activity of God accepted these new people, changed their wineskins to accommodate the Wine of God's presence, and exploded in godliness and growth. It was messy at times, but worth it.

God's movement among us now will be messy and confusing at times because people with all of our problems are messy. And it will most certainly challenge our status quo. What will drive our responses? An unhindered love of God and others or a fear of our own discomfort?

THE PROMISE

The remedy for Paul's concern was the promise of God's presence. "I am with you!" was all he needed. But the Lord followed that with a challenge and responsibility. "I have many people in this city." In other words, "Paul, you are not alone! Others will be in this great movement with you!"

And it also meant that there were many yet to be won to Christ if Paul would keep on boldly following the Spirit and sharing the gospel. If he would not cower before man's opinions. This encouragement and instruction was exactly the word Paul needed. And he "settled there a year and six months, teaching the word of God among them."

ARE YOU AFRAID?

The answer to that is quickly determined by how many people you speak to about Christ daily. If the answer is "not many" or "none," the culprit is almost always fear. We are afraid we will be persecuted, laughed at, thought less of. Or simply that it will become awkward or inconvenient with people. Or fear that we don't know what to say or are ill-equipped.

What is happening at Asbury is spreading rapidly. There are similar reports on many campuses and churches. This is precisely the same accelerated trajectory that has occurred in the last five nationwide movements in American history (First Great Awakening, 1735; Second, 1800; Prayer Revival, 1857; Welsh Revival, 1904; Jesus Movement, 1970). God has visited us every 40-60 years in America to bring the church back to Him and rapidly advance His kingdom.

It is coming to your town, your campus, and your life. In fact, it's before you right now. God is speaking with a megaphone, calling His church to fall down before Him in complete surrender and rise up in bold witness. But in the current moment sparked by the Asbury Revival, God will undoubtedly call you to enter places you may not have gone. To surrender all. To confess sin and walk deeply with Him. To worship with abandonment. To clear your conscience with those you've wronged. To give with reckless generosity. To give up your schedule. To be willing to pray all night if needed for the sake of the kingdom. And to share the gospel and testify boldly to everyone. It can be fearful.

The primary message of the Welsh revival (in which 100,000 people came to faith in nine months) was summarized in four points by Evan Roberts and others:

1. Confess all known sin

2. Lay aside every doubtful habit

3. Obey the Spirit promptly

4. Confess Christ openly

Read those four points again carefully and prayerfully. Are you willing to go there? Will you aggressively cooperate with God? Or will you turn away in fear? Will you miss God's movement or step into the powerful river of God's awakening?

> *What God in His sovereignty may yet do on the world-scale I do not claim to know, but what He will do for the plain man or woman who seeks His face I believe I do know, and can tell others. Let any man turn to God in earnest, let him begin to exercise himself unto godliness, let him seek to develop his powers of spiritual receptivity by trust and obedience and humility, and the results will exceed anything he may have hoped in his leaner and weaker days.*
>
> *AW Tozer. The Pursuit of God.*

CHAPTER 5

TARRYING

FEBRUARY 16, 2023

ONE OF THE most remarkable realities about the extraordinary spiritual movement that is happening at Asbury University is its beginning.

20 STUDENTS

After a normal chapel service on Wednesday, February 8, the speaker challenged the students to stay around if they wanted to pursue God more. Twenty students remained. Twenty. Not 200 or 2,000. Twenty. As the day wore on, they were joined by dozens more, then hundreds, then thousands in this chapel service that has now lasted for nine continuous days.

In our day of mass promotion and careful strategies, we are enamored with big. "How can we make it go viral?" "How can we get the crowd?"

The beauty of God's activity at Asbury is who God used in its initiation. He called 20 students. Not 20 faculty, 20 pastors, or 20 high-capacity Christian leaders. God moved 20 students to pursue Him, and they humbly obeyed.

WAITING

We must remember that the church of the Lord Jesus Christ, which has been unstoppable for 2,000 years, began with 12, then 120. They waited on the Lord, per His instructions, simply pursuing Him and waiting. Their activity seemed like inactivity.

> *These all with one mind were continually devoting themselves to prayer, along with the women, and Mary the mother of Jesus, and with His brothers. (Acts 1:14)*

In a matter of days, their waiting was rewarded by an invasion of God, and 3,000 people were saved in a single day.

My friend, Byron Paulus, who founded the OneCry initiative, often says, "Movements begin by not moving." Waiting on the Lord. Seeking Him. Listening for God-initiation and then aggressively cooperating with Him when He speaks, doing exactly as He directs.

Robby Gallaty, a pastor who saw 1,000 people saved in 15 weeks in his church DURING Covid, was instructed by God to sit on his porch every night and be quiet. He learned the art of waiting. God began to break him of his pride. Then, after months, God began to give instruction, which led to an explosion of spiritual harvest. It started in silence and solitude. Waiting on the Lord.

If you have the privilege of visiting Asbury during these days, you will be shocked by how quiet it often is. Hours of simple worship, interspersed by silence. There are great moments of joyful singing, testimony, preaching, joy. But there are hours through the night and early mornings of waiting on God. The room has been soaked in humble prayers for days. I wonder what would happen in our churches this Sunday if the rooms were soaked for hours in prayer.

EPHESUS

As the early church began, a new convert named Paul headed to Ephesus. He met a group of Gentile seekers who had not yet heard about all God was doing. He shared the gospel with them, the Holy Spirit came upon them (just as He had at Pentecost), and then we read this simple bit of helpful travelogue.

> When they heard this, they were baptized in the name of the Lord Jesus ... there were, in all, **about twelve men.** (Acts 19:5,7)

Twelve. (Not even twenty!) Paul continued to follow the Lord's initiation, discipling these followers. And then we read a few more amazing historical statements.

> **All** who lived in Asia heard the word of the Lord. (Acts 19:10)
>
> So the word of the Lord was **growing mightily and prevailing.** (Acts 19:20)
>
> "You see and hear that not only in Ephesus but in **almost all of Asia**, this Paul has persuaded and turned away a considerable number of people (i.e., from pagan worship) (Acts 19:26)

"I WANT REVIVAL IN MY CITY!"

Thousands are taking quick, modern-day pilgrimages to Wilmore, Kentucky, to see what God is doing. While I was there on the third day following its outbreak, I had booked a hotel room for several days but felt led to leave after three days. I went to check out, and a man was checking in.

"Are you coming for the revival?" I asked.

"Yes," he replied.

"How long are you staying?"

"Two days."

"Well, take my room. I've already paid for those days."

"That's awesome!" said the hotel receptionist.

"By the way," I asked. "Where are you from?"

"I drove ten hours from Toronto, Canada."

"That's amazing," I said. "I drove nine hours from Arkansas."

Like moths to a flame, we were drawn from north and south just like others from around the nation (and now, around the world.) God knows how to "get the crowd" when He desires to accelerate His movements and display His glory.

YOUR TOWN

Don't despise small beginnings. If you long for a spiritual movement in your life, family, church, and city, gather a few hungry believers. Like the first followers, continually devote yourselves to prayer (not promotion or programming, but prayer.) Confess all known sin, do nothing to quench the Spirit, move at His slightest promptings, and testify of what God is doing. Cry out to Him for His merciful intervention. Don't try to manipulate or make a movement, but cry to the Only-One-Who-Saves. You don't have to go to Kentucky ... Christ is in your city. You just may be one of the first twenty.

CHAPTER 6

REDEEMING A GENERATION

FEBRUARY 17, 2023

WHAT IF GOD intends to save the next generation? To redeem them from the clutches of our culture and set them ablaze for His missionary purposes? And what if Asbury is the beginning in our day?

ATLANTA

Ten years ago, a group of 50 Christian leaders met in Atlanta for a day to ask a question:

What can we do to cooperate with God to help foster revival and awakening?

The leaders of the OneCry initiative had convened this meeting, and the men in the room were well-known leaders who all shared a burning passion for the movement of God. We longed to see the next Great Awakening.

As we began that day, we went around the room, introducing ourselves by sharing when it was that each of us developed a passion for revival. As each man spoke, the vast majority traced the birth of this passion from one source: The Jesus Movement in the early 1970s. It had changed their lives and forever put a taste under their tongue for God's presence. In the spiritual fires of that visitation from God, we had all realized that more could be accomplished in five minutes of God's manifest presence than 50 years of our best human effort.

OUACHITA

Last night I was invited back to my alma mater, Ouachita Baptist University in Arkansas, to speak about what I had observed at Asbury during my recent visit. I was a freshman at OBU in 1970. On one day in the spring of 1970, God came in unusual power at a student-led noon service. The 15-minute service continued through the afternoon. All classes were canceled. Hundreds of students were overwhelmed by the manifest presence of God. God moved through that crowd that grew throughout the day, changing lives. Testimonies erupted of repentance, people clearing their consciences with those they'd wronged, salvation, humility, and brokenness.

I stood and spoke to students last night in the small chapel where that occurred and suddenly realized that day had completely changed the trajectory of my life. As a student, the next 50+ years of life and ministry were dramatically shaped by an encounter with the manifest presence of God during a season of revival and awakening.

OUR NEXT GENERATION

Our culture is overwhelmed with godlessness. We have reached a level of sexual perversion and confusion that is mind-boggling.

There is a spirit of entitlement and anarchy prevailing. Almost any small piece of news can break into a riot (just like the '60s). We want our rights, our way. It is a dangerous time for our children.

We can put acronyms and new psychological terms to it, but the best way to describe the current culture is to simply read God's description. It is found in Romans 1:18-32 where God tells us what always happens when we ignore Him, and He lifts His hand and gives us over to our own humanism. We develop "depraved minds," which means we completely lose the ability to make moral judgments. It has become, now in great measure, our collective consciousness.

The next generation is filled with the consequences of living in this environment. Depression, anger, bitterness, confusion, and sexual aberrations all stem from a Romans 1 culture. The term "mental health" is being used because there is no word to describe our students' level of loss, fear, anxiety, and confusion. They are resorting to every kind of aberrant behavior—even seeking to change their gender—trying to make sense of it all and find peace.

The tragedy is, within the next ten years, every needed pastor, missionary, godly church leader and elder will come from this hurting generation. These will be the people in charge.

WHAT IS ASBURY ABOUT?

It seems to be no coincidence that this extraordinary movement of God (that began at Asbury University but is now spreading like a rising tide to many campuses) is erupting among our next generation. What could happen if God spread this movement like a prairie fire to thousands of campuses and churches?

- What if multiplied thousands of 17-20-year-old students are genuinely saved in the next two years (just as they were in the Jesus Movement)?

- What if this is birthed, not in a nice church program, but in a moment of a radical visitation from God?

- What if it's marked (as is Asbury) by radical humility, deep repentance, aggressive obedience, and unashamed testimony?

- What if the next generation is healed from the deep dysfunctions of broken homes and commits to building godly homes that live to raise their children for Christ?

- What if this generation sees and understands the glory of God far more than their parents?

- What if a whole generation's hearts are set ablaze (just as Christ's is) for every tongue, tribe, nation, and people, and the next missionary force arises?

- What if God is interrupting our subnormal Christianity, marked by mere intellectual knowledge of Christ and little experiential relationship with the living God?

- What if our Biblical orthodoxy is ignited and informed by experiencing the manifest presence of God? If we move from knowing about God to *knowing* God, just as Paul did?

- What if the remedy for our tragic reality of plateaued and dying churches (85%) in America Is raising church men and women full of God, just like the book of Acts?

Samuel Davies was shaped by the first great awakening and later became the President of Princeton and was known as the Apostle of Virginia. He said that he saw humble pastors preach for years with little results. "Then the revival came," he said. The same pastors, Davies noted, preached the same sermons, and 200 people were saved. "The gospel became almighty," he wrote, "and carried everything before it."[3] He also said the following about the movements of God and their place in culture:

> "There are eras when only a large outpouring of the Spirit can produce a public general reformation." (Samuel Davies)[4]

GOD'S MERCIFUL INTERVENTIONS

God has given America a nationwide awakening every 40-60 years. A course correction that has radically brought us back to Him. In these times, churches have become vibrant lights for the gospel. The salt of New Testament Christianity and its morally preserving effects has returned. We must remember that "Righteousness exalts a nation, but sin is a disgrace to any people" (Proverbs 14:34)

If this is true, we should not discourage but deeply encourage the next generation's involvement in these days. We should pray that we will all not only understand God's ways in such a movement but that we will join them. That we would become participants and illustrations of what happens when a people are fully surrendered to God. Most historians believe that the Jesus Movement was far more short-lived than possible because many churches resisted

---

[3] Ian Murray, "Revival and Revivalism," Banner of Truth Trust, 1994, Carlisle, PA., Pg. 5
[4] Ibid, Pg. 21

the work among the next generation and the new wineskins it required. God helps us.

These students will make some mistakes in their zeal, but God forbid that we should seize upon a few things we don't agree with and discount the great movement of the Father redeeming a generation! The Pharisees did that and ended up crucifying the One who'd come to save them.

FINALLY ...

It is absolutely no coincidence that for over a year, the nationwide broadcast for the Collegiate Day of Prayer has been scheduled to be livestreamed from Hughes Auditorium on the campus of Asbury University this Thursday, February 23.

Next Thursday, what is happening in the sacred spot of God's visitation will be opened to everyone. Believers and churches will adopt the 4,196 American colleges and universities nationwide for laser-focused prayer. You and your church or campus can adopt a campus and join this 2-hour livestream from the auditorium in Asbury, and you can join in this day of prayer annually, the last Thursday of February.[5]

What if millions of believers united on this one day to pray for God to visit every campus with an extraordinary movement of God's Spirit that produced extraordinary results?

The providence of God has provided this. And, adding further fuel to God's fire, the "Jesus Revolution" movie (produced by Jon Erwin, whose father was radically changed by the Jesus Movement)

---

[5] Please take time to read of the amazing history of God's revivals on campuses here: https://collegiatedayofprayer.org/about/history/ It will give great perspective to you regarding what is happening right now.

premiers across America the very next day (February 24). It will be seen by millions.

God is out to save a generation. Will we cooperate? Will we pray?

CHAPTER 7

GOD'S MANIFEST PRESENCE AND OUR RESPONSE

FEBRUARY 20, 2023

IN A FEW days, the final public gatherings at Asbury will stop. In the wake of God's movement, of which Asbury was catalytic, we no longer need to look to Wilmore, Kentucky. God seems to be manifesting Himself in increasing measure in many, many places.

He may be taking our eyes off Asbury. We must realize He is near, knocking at the door of His church across our nation and world. We must ask Him to visit our lives, our churches, and our cities in power—not to pass us by.

It is to be determined how vast His movement will be. But the psalmist gives us words to describe this. He speaks of an unusual time of God's presence in Israel during the reign of a King who humbly sought the presence of God more than anything else.

God ... has made Himself known. (Psalm 48:3)

SUNDAY, FEB 19

Yesterday I heard from four different pastor-friends from Mississippi and Texas in unsolicited conversations.

Flora, MS: "A spontaneous baptism service broke out at our DNow (student retreat) last night. We baptized 52 students!"

Brandon, MS: (2:15 PM) "No words for what just happened. Leaving the church now. 104 baptized."

Arlington, Tx: "Baptized over 20 today ... (and then later) ... oops, I left too early, baptized 33"!

Longview, TX: (phone conversation)" The church met on Wednesday for prayer, and they have continued to meet (unplanned) each night for hours. On Sunday, our multiple services merged into one continuous service. 60 people were baptized on Sunday."

I'm hearing reports of people showing up at churches simply to pray for hours; churches opening their doors for people to come and pray this week throughout the day. Multiple college campuses are reporting similar ongoing meetings of prayer, repentance, and salvation.

Richard Owen Roberts describes revival as "The extraordinary movement of the Spirit of God that produces extraordinary results." How are we to explain a normal chapel service that lasts (at this point) for 11 days? Spontaneous baptisms of 251 people saved in a day in just four churches? A myriad of believers across our nation (and around the world) who are being drawn to fervent prayer and genuine repentance?

If you want to read similar accounts, read Chapter 2 of J. Edwin Orr's historical account of the 1857 revival, "The Second Evangelical Awakening." Orr was perhaps our greatest revival historian, even renowned in the secular world. He lists the actual number of attendees at noonday prayer meetings and the number converted in New York City.

"At the turn of the New Year 1858, the city of New York had a population of 850,000 people."

"In the month of February, showers of blessing had increased so much that they had become a deluge of no mean proportions. The secular press, noticing that something unprecedented was happening, began to give space to the news of the revival."

"Fulton Street, the original meeting place (for the noonday prayer gatherings) was trying to accommodate crowds by holding three simultaneous prayer meetings one above the other in rooms in the same building."

"On March 14 (Sunday) the Thirteenth Presbyterian Church of New York City received 113 by profession of faith."

"Before very long, 10,000 New Yorkers had been converted to God and were in the care of the churches and in May a good authority gave the total for the City as fifty thousand converts."

"As early as the beginning of February, 'extensive revivals ... now prevailing in the Methodist Episcopal Church all over the country' were reported ... a total of 8,000 people converted in Methodist meetings in one week."

"A Baptist journal attempted to keep abreast of the news of conversion reaching its offices, but its editor apparently gave up the task after listing 17,000 conversions reported to him by Baptist leaders in three weeks."

"The showers of blessing had caused a flood in New York, and this flood suddenly burst its bounds and swept over New England, engulfed the Ohio Valley cities and states, rolled over the newly settled West, lapped the edges of the mountains in the South, and covered the United States of America and Canada with Divine favour."

"At any rate, the number of conversions reported soon reached the total of fifty thousand weekly, a figure borne out by the fact that church statistics show an average of 10,000 additions to church membership weekly for a period of two years."

SIX RESPONSES

I was in conversation Saturday with a pastor friend, David Jett, in Mississippi. In his normal devotional time, he said, he was reading Mark 3. He texted me what he observed. This is his exact text.

One time Jesus entered a house, and the crowds began to gather again. Soon he and his disciples couldn't even find time to eat. When his family heard what was happening, they tried to take him away. "He's out of his mind," they said. But the teachers of religious law who had arrived from Jerusalem said, "He's possessed by Satan, the prince of demons. That's where he gets the power to cast out demons."

Jesus called them over and responded with an illustration. "How can Satan cast out Satan?" he asked. "A kingdom divided by civil war will collapse. Similarly, a family splintered by feuding will fall apart. And if Satan is divided and fights against himself, how can he stand? He would never survive. Let me illustrate this further. Who is powerful enough to enter the house of a strong man and plunder his goods? Only someone even stronger—someone who could tie him up and then plunder his house." (Mark 3:20-27)

The Pressures of a Move of God

When Jesus shows up and begins to move, miracles begin, and the Kingdom of God is preached. Six Groups of People begin to form:

1. **The Followers**: These are the believers that are His disciples who will be exhausted.

2. **The Hurting**: These are the lame, sick, and demonized who come pressing in out of desperation.

3. **The Familiar**: These are the ones who love us, but not the movement. They will try to protect us from ourselves.

4. **The Curious**: These will come to check out what is going on. They won't get involved, but will tell others what they have seen and what they think.

5. **The Religious:** *These come to refute and renounce the move, even calling it demonic.*

6. **The Disruptive:** *These are sent by the enemy to discourage and disrupt the move of God.*

   We must be diligent and ready to navigate through these various groups with humility to sustain a genuine move of God!

God is making Himself known. He descended upon New York City in the past. He has visited Wilmore, Kentucky, in our day. He is the same God everywhere. He longs to visit your city.

How will we respond?

CHAPTER 8

THE COMMISSIONING

FEBRUARY 24, 2023

SO WHAT WILL we do?

Sixteen days ago, a Divine voice called the students and faculty at Asbury college and seminary to Himself. It was not merely the winsome, godly preacher in their normal chapel service, Zach MeerGreebs, who called them. It was God.

At Asbury's normal chapels three days a week, they have been walking through the book of Romans. Zach was preaching through the thirty commands in Romans, Chapter 12, on how we must love each other. But he reminded them that they could do nothing without Christ. They couldn't even love right if they didn't encounter God and taste and see that He is good. They must see His love and be filled with it by the Spirit's power. They must "come to know and believe the love God has for us" (1 John 4:16).

The faithful preacher (and the God speaking through Him) called the students to tarry—to wait on God and linger at the altar. This is an unknown practice in our current Christianity and explains why we rarely see God. We will not tarry.

At first, there were 20 students, then 200, then 2000, then 20,000 and now tens of thousands, and, we pray in the coming days, millions. An estimated 100,000 seekers came through Wilmore, Kentucky, in the last two weeks from around the nation and world, seeking God. The Collegiate Day of Prayer broadcast had been planned for over a year to be aired live from Hughes auditorium. On the final night of the Asbury Awakening, through an extraordinary phenomenon, major entities picked up the broadcast sending it to multiplied millions of homes around the world on every continent.

Someone might think this phenomenon was of the student's own doing. But it was not. The Lord has drawn people from across that campus and the world to Himself. And as He drew them to Himself, the Spirit convicted them of their sin and need. And in brokenness and desperation, they tarried before the God who made them and cried out.

A Biblical note to remember: A humble, repentant cry is irresistible to God.

What has happened? Here is how the Psalmist said it in a season of the sustained presence of God in David's day ...

"God has made Himself known." (Psalm 48:3)

He has opened heaven and come down just like He's done over and over again in human history, each time His Bride has wandered from Him. He is present everywhere, all the time, but there are moments and seasons when we experience the "manifest presence" of God. Clear, unmistakable, visible, overwhelming ... so real you cannot ignore Him.

That is why the students have been overwhelmed with the lovingkindness of God.

> *We have thought on Your lovingkindness, O God, in the midst of Your temple. (Psalm 48:9)*

Their view of the King in these last weeks has been radically and eternally transformed. They trust Him now in ways they never have. They are now following Him with abandonment and joy as they've encountered the One who loves them with an everlasting love. This next generation will follow those they trust.

They have seen God's enemy flee.

> *For, lo, the kings assembled themselves. They passed by together. They saw it, then they were amazed. They were terrified, they fled in alarm (Psalm 48:4-5).*

Hundreds have testified of being released from the enemy's captivity in an instant, not through years of counseling but through a real encounter with the One who came to set the captives free. One of the wonderful leaders at Asbury told me that in one of their chapel buildings which filled daily as an overflow, the vast majority of testimonies were of addictions that were broken. It makes sense when God comes to an addicted generation.

The students and faculty have realized in 16 days that the Great Physician can heal people of every spiritual illness instantly. They have faith now to believe in His power. And they believe that He can do this for everyone because He has done it for them. This knowledge and the Spirit who inspired it have filled them with boldness, like the disciples in Acts 4.

They have repented, gladly and fully.

Your right hand is full of righteousness. (Psalm 48:10)

Why have the students at Asbury let go of the silly, worthless things they thought would give them life? Why have they turned from sin, anger, unforgiveness, and immorality? Their love of comfort and reputation and popularity? Their pride? Their addictions? All the things that—perhaps for years—they couldn't seem to release? Why have they had such a profound, Spirit-wrought change of mind that they have dropped those things gladly?

It's because God has given them a priceless gift: He has made himself known.

They have seen His righteousness and how far short they have come of the glory of God and heard His offer of deliverance. In His light, they have seen light and have run to Christ. And like the blind man whose eyes were opened and his first look was right into the eyes of Jesus, they realize they can never again go anywhere else, for He alone has the words of life.

And now, they have erupted in unceasing worship!

As is Your name, O God, so is Your praise to the ends of the earth (Psalm 48:10).

There is no description for the singing in Hughes auditorium. One of the repeating songs of these last weeks has been "You are worthy of it all." Instead of singing the sad songs of their culture, their broken past, their hurt, their confusion and depression, they are now singing the songs of the throne room of heaven!

They have worshiped the Lord and His Son continuously for 384 hours! Has anyone in their generation done that? Could they have done that? Would they have done that on their own? If someone had said, "We have a new program for you: we want you to pray without ceasing, to worship without intermission for 16 days," would they have begun and could they have continued?

No. They have been given a priceless gift. God has made Himself known to them. He has put a new song in their mouths, and they cannot be silent. It needs no programming, no fog machines or lights. It is the simple, pure, unceasing praise of those who have seen the Lord, for He has made Himself known.

WHAT'S NEXT?

I can bear witness, for I experienced this same manifest presence in 1970 on my campus when a 15-minute student-led chapel extended for hours, canceled classes, and changed our lives in an instant. I can tell these precious students what is about to happen to them, for I've been overwhelmed by it for the last 53 years.

- They will never be the same.

- They will never think the same.

- They will never be satisfied again with the things of this world.

- They will not be able to settle for merely formal religion, for that which has the form of godliness but not the power.

- They will never again be able to live a merely selfish life.

- When they are momentarily pulled back into the world—
thinking that something there can give them what they
need—they will remember His presence and will not be content until they return.

- They will find themselves reading His Word, fasting, and
praying so that they may know Him more.

I was given that gift 53 years ago, and I have never been able to
settle for anything less. I've pursued His presence for myself, my
family, the churches I've pastored, and the people I've ministered
to, for I have been taught something from the Great Teacher:

Everything flows from the presence of the Lord. Everything.

If you have Him, you have all that matters and lasts. But without
the conscious awareness of His presence, you have nothing of
value. No power, no fruit, no usefulness. Martyn Lloyd-Jones, the
powerful pastor and Welshman who loved revival, said, "There is
nothing so utterly useless as a merely formal Christian."

And that's why each time I've walked away and momentarily
thought I could go somewhere else to find life, I find myself running
back to Jesus.

God has given these precious students and faculty at Asbury,
and us all, a gift in extraordinary measure. And with no promotion
or advertising, He is now giving that gift to multitudes.

Staggering reports are coming in of the broad reach of this
news of this Divine Invasion. That's why thousands flocked to
Wilmore, Kentucky. That's why Hughes auditorium has been
marked not only by glorious singing but also by quietness. The

Bible calls this "awe." It is always present when God comes. "The Lord is in His holy temple. Let all the earth keep silent." The King has come.

THE REALIZATION

2 Kings, Chapter 7 records the story of God's people who were surrounded by an overwhelming army. Their food was cut off, and they were dying. The prophet, Elijah, proclaimed, "Tomorrow, you will have all the food you need." An unbelieving skeptic said, "Behold, if the Lord should make windows in heaven, could this thing be?" Then he said, "Behold, you will see it with your own eyes, but you will not eat of it" (2 Kings 7:2). This is always true of the proud: they may see the activity of God around them, but they will never experience it.

Four lepers were sitting at the gate and said, "Why should we sit here until we die?" If we go into the city, we're going to die, and if we sit here, we're going to die. Let's go to the camp of our enemy."

When they did, they found that God had routed the enemy. In the enemy's haste and confusion, they left everything. They began to devour the food and take the spoils of God's victory. Then one said, "We are not doing right. This day is a day of good news, but we are keeping silent. Let us get up and go to our city and tell."

My brother, Tom, once called this the story of the sitters, the getters, and the goers and tellers. All of us are in one of these categories.

THE COMMISSIONING

Consider her ramparts; God through her palaces that you may tell it to the next generation. For such is God; our God forever and ever. (Psalm 48:13-14)

The calling to all these in Asbury and elsewhere is to turn our eyes now from Wilmore, Kentucky. We are to look back to our cities and see those who are starving. To realize our children and grandchildren, and friends and neighbors are dying a slow, painful death without the Bread of the Presence. How can they know unless someone tells them there is a bountiful, never-ending feast that is a repentant prayer away? That God has everything before them because everything flows from His presence?

The students of Asbury and all to whom God is making Himself known are being called by God not to just stay at the table but to go home and tell. We don't have to be elaborate or gifted, or gloriously articulate. We don't have to be greatly educated. Like the New Testament disciples, who the religious snobbery labeled as "uneducated and untrained men," we must simply tell of the God we've seen—the old, old story of Jesus and His love.

As a pastor, a mom or dad, or a member of His body of which He is the head: He is laying His hand on us to go and tell ... and something more. He is calling us to embrace this gift coming through His Divine visitation on the next generation. It will call for new wineskins. It will call us to let some things go. They will make some mistakes (that's why we are there to graciously disciple them, and also learn from them). We must live for those behind us. To pass the baton. This outpouring is spreading to multiple college campuses and churches. God is healing this generation so He can use them in the next decades.

And here's a sobering Biblical warning: Don't quench the Spirit. Many churches did not receive what God was doing in 1970. They rejected the work of God because it was uncomfortable to release some things into the hands of those younger, those who were seeing God and overwhelmed with joy.

Our leaders and churches could do the same. We could miss the work of God, not only for ourselves and our churches but perhaps for our own children and grandchildren. There could be nothing more grievous.

God is calling us to embrace His fresh wind. Examine everything carefully, just as 1 Thessalonians 5 says, but not with preconceived opinions, hearsay information, and the arrogant desire to make your point. Tarry before God (not social media) and pray that God will make Himself known to you—and your children and your church—because everything flows from the presence of the Lord. Everything.

And for all in the next generation ... not only a human hand, but GOD'S hand is now on your shoulders, commissioning you. And know this: the hands of millions of adults are on you and beneath you; millions who believe in God and believe in you. He is now commissioning you. He's telling you to take your eyes off Asbury and look at the people around you who are dying without Christ. With a broken heart and wet eyes, you must not be a sitter or a self-absorbed getter but a goer and a teller. It's time!

You have received the greatest gift of all: His presence. And the rest of your life must be spent enjoying Him and telling others that there is MORE.

CHAPTER 9

RESPONDING IN OUR CHURCH AND CAMPUS

FEBRUARY 27, 2023

REVIVAL IS THE necessary, extraordinary movement of the Holy Spirit that produces extraordinary results. God is always moving. We could not rise out of bed without His grace. In Him, we live, move, and have our being.

But there are moments when God deems it necessary to open the windows of Heaven and manifest Himself in extraordinary ways. He does this because of His merciful love for His Bride who often goes astray. But he also revives His church to move us to the task the world needs. His Body, which He created and leads, gets distracted by the bangles of the world and the busyness of life.

We often lose sight of our great task to be the conduit for Christ to lost people. In revival, God makes Himself known, we see Him and are changed, and He ignites a fresh passion for His agenda: to seek and save those who are lost.

DRAWN

When He manifests Himself in unusual measure, hungry, hurting people are drawn to Christ like moths to a flame. It has always been this way.

> *Jesus withdrew to the sea with His disciples, and a great multitude from Galilee followed; and also from Judea, and from Jerusalem, and from Idumea, and beyond the Jordan, and the vicinity of Tyre and Sidon, **a great number of people heard of all that He was doing and came to Him.** (Mark 3:7-8).*

We have just witnessed this at Asbury and elsewhere as it spreads. Christ has shown up in power, doing the miraculous things He does, and people are drawn to Him. They find a way—often at great cost and inconvenience—to get to Jesus.

It is our great prayer that this extraordinary movement will spread like a raging fire across our nation and world. So how do we aggressively cooperate with God to see that happen in our church, campus, and city?

PURSUE CHRIST, NOT A CROWD

We cannot use the same humanistic methods we have used in the past to try to build attendance and gather a crowd. In fact, we don't need to.

Hughes chapel and the overflow venues were packed with thousands of people in a few days. People came from around the world. And the social media posts are (some reports say) in the billions. But the genesis of this extraordinary attention has been humble, broken people pursuing Christ and Christ alone. They weren't planning to "have a meeting" designed to attract a crowd or create a social media buzz through deliberate strategy.

They waited before the Lord. They tarried, longing for Him. They humbled themselves, Christ came in power ... and the crowd came in thousands. Look through the history of the five Great Awakenings in American history. They all began with a few people who prayed, fasted, repented and looked to Jesus because they knew only Christ could bring what was needed.

Remember Pentecost? A small band of men and women waited with one mind in prayer, and the Spirit came in power. There just "happened to be" people from "every nation under heaven" who were present as the outpouring occurred and the gospel was shared in power. God knows how to draw the crowd to get His message out.

OPERATE WITH RADICAL HUMILITY, NOT PRIDE

Pride is unbelievably subtle and the foundational weapon in Satan's arsenal. I regularly ask those I serve with to point pride out when they see its ugly head rising in my life. I often can't see it. You can live in pride in such ways that it drives everything you do. It seems natural and right because very few contrasting examples exist in those around you. When you encounter a deeply humble person, the contrast is stark, unsettling, and convicting.

You must learn to discern the enemy's voice. For me, it's a constant whisper that I must quickly resist. "Read that social media post you wrote and see how many people are responding." "Steer the conversation to what you have done." "Make sure they know that you were responsible for that." "Don't obey the prompting the Spirit just gave you ... what will people think?"

It is nauseous how incessantly Satan whispers. But, if we are a child of God, we can resist this deadly voice in our ears. But we must keep resisting every thought that stems from pride. Satan pestered Christ in the wilderness three times until He realized He would not entertain proud suggestions. He left Him, deciding to wait for a "more opportune time" to return.

When you hear the enemy's whispers, instantly rebuke him in Christ's name. "Resist the devil, and he will flee from you," God promises (James 4:7).

CHANGE YOUR WINESKINS TO MAKE ROOM FOR CHRIST

And He told His disciples that a boat should stand ready for Him because of the crowd, so that they would not crowd Him, for He had healed many, with the result that all those who had afflictions pressed around Him in order to touch Him. (Mark 3:9-10)

Under Divine instructions, the disciples pivoted to make room for more people to see and hear Christ. (Please read that sentence again, humbly, prayerfully).

Few people realize what was happening behind the scenes to accommodate the activity of God at Asbury. In an insightful article entitled "No Celebrities But Jesus: How Asbury Protected Revival," the writer tells us of the humble service and leadership provided by the Asbury leaders and volunteers to make room for the 16 days of non-stop worship.

An ad hoc revival committee of about seven people gathered in the one quiet space in Hughes—a storage closet. According to several people who were there, they pushed aside a drum kit and keyboard and sat knee to knee. Someone found a dry-erase board, and they asked each other, "What are we going to do in the next two hours?"

Then they started thinking slightly longer term: "Will students stay all night? What does that look like? Should we leave the sound system on? Should we let students keep bringing guitars into chapel?"

... Other decisions they made in the next few days seem, as the ad hoc committee reflects on them now, almost like they happened by instinct. There was no time for drawn-out discussions. They would meet in the storage closet and make decisions minute by minute. Did they want to put up screens for the lyrics of the worship songs? No. Should ministers who spoke on stage stop to introduce themselves? No. Should they put up signs asking people not to livestream? Yes.

"We were just trying to keep up," student life vice president Sarah Thomas Baldwin told CT. "There are people and they're showing up, and they're desperate for God. We're just trying to stay alive and trying to honor what is happening."

The group decided to have ministers stay in Hughes and have security watch the building but keep it open.

They would let the students stay and pray and sing as long as they wanted. The group quickly came to a consensus that they hadn't started the outpouring, hadn't planned any of this, but they were nonetheless called in that moment to be hospitable. They would work to host it and hold it, all the while keeping in mind that they were not in control.

"There was a tension," Brown told CT, "between 'How do we maintain orderliness?' and 'How do we create space for this spiritual unfolding that we haven't planned, we don't know where it's heading, but we know it's good and bigger than us?' "[6]

I have talked with many pastors in the last few days who long to see God manifest Himself in their churches. My counsel to them is not to try to manipulate or create anything but to aggressively seek Him and make room for Him.

Have special prayer meetings as God directs. Follow the Biblical model that led to Pentecost in Acts 1:14. Open the worship center all day for those who want to pray. Remind your people at the first of Sunday services that your only agenda is to pursue Christ and that the altar is open every moment for them to come, even during your sermon. Be willing to adjust your schedule during a service as He leads.

Gather a group early on Sunday morning and soak the building in fervent prayer and worship. Worship longer. Pray longer. And most of all, forget about the silly convention we call a "clock" and

---

[6] Daniel Steelman, *"No Celebrities But Jesus: How Asbury Protected Revival,"* Christianity Today, Feb. 23, 2023.

operate on God's timetable alone. It seems that one of the things that God is calling us to do is to tarry. To wait on Him. Be willing to change any wineskins to accommodate the extraordinary Wine of His presence. Most importantly, walk by the Spirit. Make decisions and adjustments by God-initiation alone.

And you must pursue Him personally. I find myself lately singing the simple song penned by Fanny Crosby over and over again. "Pass me not, oh gentle Savior. Hear my humble cry. While on others thou art calling, do not pass me by."

Preach the gospel fervently, for it will be attended with unusual power in these days of God's awakenings. One young girl at Baylor stood on a chair in the cafeteria last week to proclaim the gospel. We are hearing stories of people coming off the street to find Christ. Be ready and seize Divine opportunities and remember that the unashamed, bold proclamation of the gospel is the power of God unto salvation to all who believe.

Cry out to God and wait on Him. And then stand still and see the salvation of the Lord.

CHAPTER 10

GOD'S WAYS IN REVIVAL

FEBRUARY 28, 2023

THE EXTRAORDINARY MOVEMENT that has happened at Asbury in the last weeks has had many commentators. Thousands are beside themselves with joy and hope, for they sense that God is answering their prayers (some who've prayed for decades.) But there are many skeptics also, and some who are adamantly opposed and unbelieving about this unusual activity of God.

One man recently remarked to a friend of mine that he didn't believe in the concept of "revival" and movements of spiritual awakening. And furthermore, that he didn't need it. He was very content with what he received at church every Sunday and was fully satisfied with the simple, routine life of normal Christianity.

THE WAYS OF GOD

I understand what this man is saying. My life has been fueled and built day by day for 71 years by meeting each morning with Christ through the word and prayer, submitting to His leadership, regularly repenting, gathering with other believers for growth and worship and ministry, preaching His life-changing Word of God, and hearing it proclaimed. The God-given means of spiritual life are what develop us all.

But to not believe in the extraordinary, unusual movements of God, indicates one doesn't understand the ways of God in Scripture and human history.

When God manifested Himself in human flesh, He used the miraculous to accelerate faith and glorify Himself. Study the story of Jesus forgiving and healing the paralytic lowered through the roof to the feet of Jesus by his friends, (which I read in my daily reading this morning).

> And he got up and immediately picked up the pallet and went out in the sight of everyone, so that they were all amazed and were glorifying God, saying, "We have never seen anything like this." And He went out again by the seashore; and all the people were coming to Him, and He was teaching them. (Mark 2:12-13)

Notice the end result of this supernatural work of God through His Son.

- They were all amazed.

- They were glorifying God.

- They commented that they had "never seen anything like this before." It was unusual and extraordinary.

- All the people were coming to Him (the crowd grew).

- And Jesus was teaching them (the gospel extended). An opportunity for an even greater witness was realized.

All of these results are what every true believer should long for in every generation, unless, of course, their Christianity is more narrow. If the only thing they are concerned about is their own personal religion and not the rapid expansion of Christ's kingdom on earth. God used the extraordinary and unexplainable in Jesus' ministry not only to bless people in need, and to validate His Son, but to glorify Himself and advance His kingdom.

HIS WAYS IN HISTORY

To not believe in extraordinary seasons of revival and spiritual awakening is to be unaware of our Bibles and church history. It seems one should be careful before coming to such a conclusion and making such statements (which could affect the fragile faith of others and perhaps cause us to miss something God intends). Look at American history alone, and you will see at least five unquestionable seasons of spiritual awakening, mercifully given by God every 40-60 years.

1. **The first Great Awakening in the 1730-1740's** in which 15% of the population of America came to faith in Christ. The pastors of several towns said that they could find no adult in their town who had not become a believer.

2. **The second Great Awakening in the early 1800's.** One reputable historian says that this extended season of revival shaped America more than any period in American history.[7] Churches, schools, hospitals, and religious organizations

---

[7] Conversation with Mark Noll of Regent University and previously of Notre Dame with Bob Bakke

were begun and tens of thousands saved, providing a course correction to the nation and the rapid advance of the gospel.

3. **The 1857-1858 Prayer revival,** in which 50,000 people were gathering for prayer every workday at the noon hour in New York City alone. Reliable records tell us that 10,000 people a week were added to church membership every week for two years.[8] Out of an American population of 30 million, 1 million came to faith in 24 months.

4. **The Welsh Revival of 1904-1905,** which dramatically impacted America and many nations around the world. 100,000 people came to faith in this small principality slightly smaller than New Jersey, and the revival spread to "the rest of Britain, Scandinavia, parts of Europe, North America, India, the Orient, Africa, and Latin America.[9]

5. **The Jesus Movement of the early 1970's,** which was dramatically catalyzed by a similar movement in 1970 at Asbury, a chapel service that extended seven days. The records of one of America's largest denominations (Southern Baptists) show that more students came to Christ in 1970-71 than any period before or since.

Such seasons are the *necessary*, habitual work of God. We can deduce this is true because God keeps repeating such movements! It is necessary because of the church's tendency to fall away, losing our first love. Study Christ's words to the churches in Revelation.

---

[8] J. Edwin Orr, "The Second Great Evangelical Awakening," Purnell and Sons, Great Britain, 1955, Chapter 2

[9] J. Edwin Orr, "The Flaming Tongue," Moody Press, Chicago, IL., 1973, Pg. 28

There is an undeniable Biblical and historical cycle of the church falling away, God bringing His needed judgment and discipline, the church coming to desperation and a united, repentant cry—a rising tide of prayer—followed by extraordinary interventions from heaven as God revives His people and brings spiritual awakening among the lost.

EXCESSES

There have been broad reports of excesses that happened at Asbury that are simply not true. I was sitting in the room for five of the 16 days. I have talked with the leaders and observed their humble, wise leadership. This continuous, 16-day movement was marked by extreme humility, fervent prayer, overflowing worship, simple, Biblical preaching (every night), and glorious testimonies of changed lives. And, it seems to be continuing on many campuses and churches, and we all pray that it will.

I do not know this young lady (J. Madison Pierce) who made the following observations on social media. But her observations are insightful.

> I am a 25-year-old seminary student at Asbury. I have participated in the meetings at Asbury movement since the beginning. I've been hesitant to post my thoughts since I find we often get lost in the wrong conversation talking about "revival." Despite this, it seems that God is moving in a surprising way for Gen Z. I find it interesting that God would mark this particular outpouring with:

- A tangible sense of peace for a generation with unprecedented anxiety.

- A restorative sense of belonging for a generation amidst an epidemic of loneliness.

- An authentic hope for a generation marked by depression and suicidal ideation.

- A leadership emphasizing protective humility in relationship with power for a generation deeply hurt by the abuse of religious power.

- A focus on participatory adoration in an age of digital distracted.

It feels as if God is personally meeting young adults in ways meaningful to my generation. A generation formed differently than previous so the traits of this outpouring are different than revivals of old. The new outpouring is not the signs and wonders nor zealous intercession nor spontaneous tongues nor charismatic physicalities nor the weeping wails. It is marked by a tangible feeling of holistic peace, a restorative sense of belonging, a non-anxious presence through felt safety, repentance driven by experienced kindness, humble stewardship of power, and holiness through treasuring adoration.

It would not surprise me if any revival had some excesses (most do), but the accusations coming from many regarding Asbury are usually from those who were not there. Every true revival and awakening in history has had some excesses. Revival can be messy because we are messy.

But does the presence of some excesses mean that a true movement of God is not happening? G. Campbell Morgan, the brilliant and godly pastor of Westminster Chapel and predecessor of Martyn Lloyd-Jones said of the Welsh revival:

> *"In what seemed supreme confusion, one was conscious of splendid order ... It was a meeting characterized by a perpetual series of interruptions and disorderliness; it was a meeting characterized by a great continuity and absolute order."*[10]

Others commented that the Welsh revival was marked by ...

> *"The sovereignty of the Holy Spirit in all His operations, the possibility of Spirit-filled assembly, confidence in the inspired Word of God, the power of earnest, united prayer, and the power of sacred song—these were the marks of this revival.*

Another observer summarized (the Welsh Revival):

1. *Honor to the Holy Spirit as a presiding presence.*

2. *The plain preaching of Christ and of sound gospel doctrine.*

3. *The prominence given to prayer, individual and united.*

---

[10] J. Edwin Orr, "The Flaming Tongue," Moody Press, Chicago, IL., 1973, Pg. 28

4. *The dependence upon God, rather than upon men.*

5. *The absence of stereotyped program and set method.*

6. *The readiness for blessing by a willingness to remove obstacles.*

7. *The direct dealing with the unconverted."*[11]

EXAMINE EVERYTHING CAREFUL

Paul reminds us not to quench the Holy Spirit or despise (treat lightly, flippantly) when God speaks. He also wisely reminds us to examine everything carefully, hold onto the good, and reject what is false (1 Thessalonians 5:19-20). I have seen some supposed "revivals" that did not seem to follow Biblical patterns and were primarily fueled by excesses. In my humble opinion, what has happened inside Hughes Auditorium at Asbury University does not in any way fall into this category.

Examine what God is doing now carefully. But not from a proud, judgmental heart. Don't judge the whole work of God— which we all pray would sweep our desperately needed nation and world and bring renewal, reformation, and gospel harvest—by any excesses on the fringes. Don't be guilty of using one supposed excess reported as a proof-text for your concerns.

Our great passion should be to help the next generation see that the Church for which Christ died is not a dry, lifeless organization. Our children have been walking away from such churches in droves, and the culture shows the loss. But let's personally repent and cry out so that they will see a church alive with the supernatural

---

[11] Ibid., Pg. 14, 20

power of God. Let's pray they will be able to echo the benediction of Paul.

Now to Him who is able to do far more abundantly beyond all that we ask or think, according to the power that works within us, to Him be the glory in the church and in Christ Jesus to all generations forever and ever. Amen. (Ephesians 3:20-23)

CHAPTER 11

WHAT IS GOD DOING?

MARCH 5, 2023

TEN DAYS AGO the doors were closed at midnight in Hughes Auditorium at Asbury University. It was the final service open to the public in what had been an unbelievable 16-day, 24-hour-a-day invasion of God upon the campus. Students came from over 250 campuses across the nation out of their thirst for God. The final Collegiate Day of Prayer broadcast went to millions across the world.

But is the revival over? The massive attention on social media about Asbury has slowed. To those whose only source is such media, it might seem so.

But nothing could be further from the truth. My brother, Tom, told me recently, "Dissolution is often about dissemination." Read Acts 8:4. All attention had been on the extraordinary work of God in Jerusalem. Tens of thousands had come to Christ in short order. But persecution arose, and the Christians scattered and went everywhere preaching the Word of God. Dissolution for greater dissemination. The gospel extended from one city to the whole world.

Although the thousands are not converging each night in Wilmore, Kentucky, a far greater movement is happening in an innumerable number of colleges and churches. These reports are not as dramatic as Asbury, and many are in different shapes and forms. But there is an undeniable stirring happening everywhere. Like a tsunami that travels miles underground and explodes on the shore, the rising tide is building.

Those who love Christ and long for His work are experiencing a heightened sense of His presence. Worship services are extending. Prayer meetings—both large and small—are happening in high schools, colleges, churches, and small groups. And reports are coming in of an unusual number of conversions happening, 30-60-100 fold. It's still embryonic in light of history but seems to be a cloud the size of a man's hand. The fascinating thing is that reports are coming from everywhere.

My brother, Tom, met last week with a group of men he's prayed with for 38 years. He simply shared about what God was doing. When it was time for a brief prayer time (usually given to everyone's concerns for routine issues), no one moved. They were in awe of what God was doing. The leader got up to dismiss the group, but they would not leave and it led to a fervent time in God's presence and prayers for revival and awakening.

One of our church staff members sent us a note yesterday from Hawaii, where she was on an anniversary trip.

> *"Just got to the beach in Hawaii for the first time and watched several college students get baptized in the ocean! I think it was 20 or more before it stopped! They are still out there singing hymns to the Lord! God is on the move!"*

TAKING STOCK

Henry Blackaby and Claude King, in their historic study, "Experiencing God," said that we must "find out where God is moving and join Him." Aggressive cooperation with God is the daily recipe for a godly life, but in days of God's extraordinary movement, our spiritual ears should be even more highly attuned to His activity. What is God doing, and how can we join Him? Notice five observable movements.

1. GOD IS REVEALING HIMSELF

Revival is nothing more nor less than God making Himself known. We refer to this as His manifest presence. In days of revival, He chooses to do this in ways that even the unbelieving can see.

The headline of the Denver Post during the 1857-58 nationwide revival that was marked by tens of thousands stopping everywhere to unite in prayer daily and 1 million people coming to Christ in two years read:

ENTIRE CITY PAUSES TO PRAY EVEN AT THE HIGH TIDE OF BUSINESS AS THE SOUL RISES ABOVE SORDID THOUGHTS
Remarkable Outburst of Gospel Sentiment Provoked by Revival

In days of His extraordinary movements, He shows Himself with stunning clarity, and a nationwide awakening flows from millions of fresh encounters with the Author and Finisher of our faith. It seems that the pathway to this fresh revelation of God is to tarry, to wait on Him, and to look to Him. Don't look to a method or formula. Look to Jesus and settle for nothing less than a fresh, life-changing encounter with Him.

Do you long to know Him? Is your soul thirsty for His presence in such ways that you will do anything to experience Him? To fall in love with Him all over again?

2. GOD IS REVIVING HIS CHILDREN

To "revive" means to "bring to life again." In the light of God's manifest presence, we see (just as the students experienced at Asbury) the astounding beauty of the Lord. We are in awe of his glory and humbled by His holiness. When this occurs, we will find ourselves gladly repenting. Repentance becomes a glad delight, not an arduous duty. And such an encounter with God brings repentance without regrets.

This is why those at Asbury sang with utter abandonment for 16 days. Standing in Hughes auditorium on that final night, I was so caught up in worship that I could hardly speak. When the gospel was presented, I watched many stand with joy to believe and confess Him, and their friends running across the room to embrace their new brothers and sisters in Christ. Others bowed low in worship, washing their Redeemer's feet with their tears.

Isn't this what you long for? Or are you content with merely formal Christianity? If COVID did anything for us, it showed us that we are powerless to control anything and that the world's fare doesn't touch the deepest longings of our souls. Only Jesus can save us, and He is doing that across the nation at increasing speed.

Are you repenting? Is there a fresh hunger to do anything God says so that you can be right before God and man? Are you keeping the roof off and walls down?

3. GOD IS REFORMING HIS CHURCH

Many are saying we need reformation, not revival. It is a false dichotomy. How could we have one without the other? Although I have lived and died for the correct handling of the Word of God for over 50 years, it seems the great need for our dying churches is not merely Biblical orthodoxy but a reformation of experiential religion. We need a reformation of our wineskins that will open the door for the King of Glory to come in. We need a reformation in the church that will include ...

- A reformation of **PRAYER**

- A reformation of **INSTANT OBEDIENCE TO GOD'S WORD**

- A reformation of **HUMBLE LEADERSHIP**

- A reformation of **SPIRIT-FILLED DEPENDENCE**

- A reformation of **TRANSPARENT REPENTANCE AND CONFESSION**

- A reformation of **REGULAR TESTIMONY**

- A reformation of **SPIRIT-LED, UNPRODUCED WORSHIP**

- A reformation of **GOD-INITIATED (EVEN SPONTANEOUS) MOVEMENT, NOT ROUTINE PROGRAMMING**

- A reformation of **RADICAL GENEROSITY**

- A reformation of **UNASHAMED WITNESSING**

- A reformation of **UNCEASING ATTENTION TO HIS PRESENCE!**

- A reformation of **AWE AND AMAZEMENT** (which is mentioned 95 times in the New Testament)

Are you ready for this type of reformation? Are you tired of business as usual and longing to see your life and church described by the words of Acts? A reformation where God is experienced and known and glorified and the kingdom advances with accelerated power?

4. GOD IS REDEEMING A GENERATION

The next generation is marked by incredible confusion and anxiety. They do not know if they are men or women. There seem to be more addictions than at any time in history. Even unbelievers are astounded by the level of "mental health" issues in homes and schools. All of our best education and medical solutions are not touching the acceleration of suicide and self-harm.

Revival changes that. As I sat in Hughes auditorium, day after day, and heard testimony after testimony of radically, instantly changed lives by the power of God, I realized something important about what God was doing.

Every pastor, missionary, educator, politician, medical worker, mom, dad, and businessman this world needs is coming out of this next generation. They are worse than ill-prepared to lead with their current emotional and spiritual dysfunction. But a nationwide movement of revival could bring healing in an instant. It can (and has) redeemed not only individuals in the past but whole segments of society. God wants to change a generation for their sake and for the generation that will follow them. This is why God has sent nationwide awakenings in America every 40-60 years—every generation.

My brother, Jim, wrote recently ...

> If you told me that the young adults in your church
> were meeting together for long periods of time daily
> to repent of sin, exalt Christ, sing worshipfully, read
> Scripture, hear at least one message daily, tell others
> about Christ, give and receive many scriptural exhor-
> tations, and to fully enjoy the Lord, (even if there is
> some immaturity here or there) I would be ecstatic!
>
> And, then, I would also encourage you to mentor all
> who would be interested, learn and listen to them, an-
> swer questions, guide, speak the gospel clearly, teach
> the nature of conversion to Christ, instruct about true
> and false conversion, the walk in the Spirit, freedom
> from sin and contagious joy in Christ. In other words,
> I would say, "Walk in the Spirit and with the Spirit in
> what He is doing. Don't miss this amazing moment."

*Are you interested—really passionate about—the next generation? Do
you see how critical it is to pray unceasingly for them and for the kind
of spiritual movements that would redeem them, heal them, and propel
them to Jesus and fervent ministry with Him? And are you willing to
live with their weaknesses (as they have lived with yours and mine since
birth) and help them to greater godliness? And are we ready to release
ministry into their hands so they can learn and grow just as we did?*

4. GOD IS RAISING AN ARMY!

If you study revival history, you will notice God's endgame. It is prov-
able that almost every great acceleration of missionary activity has

come after seasons of revival and awakening. The Moravian missionaries sprang from the Moravian "Pentecost," as it was called, as God interrupted a normal Sunday with an unusual outpouring. This led to a 100-year prayer meeting and our first modern missionaries who left their shores with their worldly goods packed in coffins, planning never to return. William Carey sprang from the Second Great Awakening, as did the Haystack Prayer Meeting of 1806 that launched the Student Volunteer movement and the rise of American missions.

God loves His children and manifests Himself so they may return to Him. And as they respond in repentance and humility, their hearts begin to beat in unison with His. And His heart is for people from every tongue, tribe, nation, and people.

Could it be that the result of a world being completely shut down during the COVID pandemic has led to worldwide desperation? Could this lead to a worldwide cry to the only One who can save us and a worldwide spiritual awakening? And could this—oh, Father, we pray!—lead to the greatest missionary force being raised in human history that could reach every tribe, tongue, nation, and people and then the end would come? We do not know, of course, but can we pray to that end?

Are you concerned about missions? About a lost world? If you are, you must not criticize something that seems to have the potential of a national, perhaps worldwide, spiritual movement that could result in the salvation of millions. Even with any excesses on the fringes, we should cry out to God to continue and raise the next great missionary force to finish God's great Kingdom agenda.

AND YOU ...

Every nationwide spiritual awakening has been experienced by millions but also missed by millions. There are many who will discount what is happening and even seek to abort it. The phenomena of social media could be used by God to rapidly advance revival, but also used by the Enemy to rapidly discredit it and seek to stop the activity of God.

He is standing at the door of your life and your home and your church knocking, just as He was to the Laodicean church in Revelation 3:20.

Will you open the door to the One who loves you more than His own life, and will you do it today?

CHAPTER 12

PERSONAL REVIVAL

MARCH 7, 2023

WE HAVE ALL observed the extraordinary movement of God in the last thirty days, highlighted by the sixteen days of non-stop worship at Asbury University. It seems to be spreading across America, incrementally but significantly, to college campuses and local churches. It's not an all-consuming tidal wave yet, but a rapidly rising tide. If you know Christ, your heart is optimistic that what is happening could be the beginning of a nationwide spiritual awakening—a movement of God we desperately need.

One of my dearest friends that I've pastored for 40 years wrote to me this week. This retired 86-year-old physician said that he had followed what was happening at Asbury and read carefully all that was occurring. But then he said, "I still had not been able to experience personal revival in my life as I so wanted."

We all have our responses to what's happened. Some may ignore or even criticize, but most Christians are asking, "What about my church, my campus, Lord?" And, more humbly, "What about me?"

CORPORATE OR PERSONAL?

If revival is the "extraordinary movement of the Spirit of God that produces extraordinary results," we must ask, "Is revival corporate or personal?" "Is it for a group of people or for me?" And the answer, of course, is ... YES!

Everything that happens with a group of people must happen, first and foremost, with individuals. I listened today to an 8-minute video describing the Asbury awakening. It was the testimonies of students, one by one, who had encountered God. The overwhelming summary of those testimonies was that God had visited their campus. It has been a merciful outpouring of His manifest presence. Salvation, healing, reconciliation, and deliverance from sin and addictions has happened rapidly. But it has been personal to each of them. They were faced individually with what they would do as they beheld the glory of the Lord ... and they cooperated with Him and were radically changed.[12]

WHY DO WE NEED REVIVAL, AND WHERE IS IT FOUND?

You can use whatever terms you desire, but the great tragedy of our day is that we have never encountered Christ or that we have drifted from the Christ we know.

Mark 10 records the story of the rich young ruler who had everything but one thing: life. "What shall I do to inherit eternal life?" he asked. Jesus knew the real issue. He told him to walk away from what he thought would give him life (his possessions) and follow the only One who could give him life. "Come, follow

---

[12]Listen to their testimonies here: https://www.youtube.com/watch?v=fJ wQSEihmhQ)

Me," Jesus simply said. The man was so convinced that his worldly idol was necessary that he walked away from Jesus.

Spiritual awakening comes when God stands before you, offering you life for the first time or the 1,000[th] time. It is not found in a formula, a particular type of worship expression, or six simple steps. If you want life, you must come to Jesus. "Where else can we go?" Peter said, "for you have the words of eternal life" (John 6:68).

All true Christians drift. Christ describes all of us as He speaks to the seven churches in Revelation 2-3. Some of us are orthodox, but we don't love Jesus anymore. Our intimacy with Him has evaporated. Others are proud and think they need nothing. Others have gotten turned by some false teaching. Some have allowed subtle compromises and tolerations to pull us away from Jesus. Many are apathetic, asleep, or lukewarm. Take your pick. We all live there more than we'd admit, and our lives, homes, and churches show the results of our lack of intimacy with Christ.

Read through Christ's prescription for these churches and individuals (us), summed up in one repeated word: repent. We must turn from what has consumed us. We must come back, not to a system or a program, but to Christ. He alone has life. He's standing at the door, knocking, waiting for access.

AND IF ...

Some are hesitant to sit quietly before the searchlight of God's word and Spirit and let Him evaluate us. But if we seek Him, He will let us find Him. And when we humbly bow at His feet again and fall in love with Him all over again, the reward is spectacular. It is described to us by David in Psalm 65.

He will hear our prayers.

> *O You who hear prayer, to You all men come. (Psalm 65:2)*

You will not find Him too busy or unconcerned. You also will not encounter a stern God whose great delight is to punish a thirsty seeker. As you humbly come, you will be overwhelmed by the beauty of His holiness, lovingkindness, and mercy. You will find Him waiting. He loves you and wants to talk with you. In fact, He has given His own Son so that you can stand with peace facing Him and enjoy this "grace in which we now stand" (Romans 5:1-2).

He is listening. Will you come to Him? Cry out to Him? Pray with no intermission? Wait in silence before Him? Seek Him with all your heart? Will you tarry until all impediments are gone, and you are deeply aware of His presence?

He will forgive our sins.

> *Iniquities prevail against me. As for our transgressions,*
> *You forgive them. (Psalm 65:3)*

There is no weight heavier, no disease deadlier, and no chain tighter than the sin we experience as we walk away from Him. He longs to cleanse us and liberate us. To remove the chains and heal the scars. You can run everywhere, trying to assuage the guilt and the pain of your sin. Or, you can seek Him honestly, transparently, and fully and let Him forgive, cleanse, and restore.

Are you willing to admit your sin and acknowledge your need? When was the last time you let the Great Physician do a complete spiritual exam? And are you ready to let go of the things you've been turning to for life and come follow Jesus?

He will give us the gift of His presence.

> How blessed is the one whom You choose and bring near
> to You to dwell in Your courts. (Psalm 65:4)

There is no greater joy, no greater delight than Him. "In Your presence is fullness of joy," David sang. The believer is indwelt by God's Spirit. But we all know that we can have His Spirit but His Spirit not have us in full measure. That's why we were given the command to be continually filled (controlled, dominated, consumed) with His Spirit. Sin interrupts this filling, and we lose the conscious awareness and essential empowering of His presence.

Are you experiencing Him in such ways that you are filled with joy? Have you been grieving or quenching His Spirit? Have you lost the joy of His salvation, and you feel as if He is distant? Are you willing to do whatever is necessary to draw near to the Lord? If you will, He will draw near to you.

Our hearts will be completely satisfied.

> We will be satisfied with the goodness of Your house, Your
> holy temple. (Psalm 65:4)

C.S. Lewis pursued academics with a passion but finally realized there was only one place his soul could be made happy.

> God made us: invented us as a man invents an engine.
> A car is made to run on petrol, and it would not run
> properly on anything else. Now God designed the
> human machine to run on Himself. He Himself is the
> fuel our spirits were designed to burn, or the food our
> spirits were designed to feed on. There is no other.

That is why it is just no good asking God to make us happy in our own way without bothering about religion. God cannot give us a happiness and peace apart from Himself, because it is not there. There is no such thing.[13]

OUR RESPONSE

I read an article by a well-respected Christian writer as he commented about the current movement at Asbury and beyond. I respect this man and have been blessed by his teaching in the past. But I was surprised and saddened by his response. Unless I'm misreading, (and I could be), he seemed dismissive of what is happening. He wrote,

> "You don't need to care about everything. You don't need to take an interest in everything. You don't need to have an opinion on everything. You certainly don't need to voice your opinion on everything. If a situation like that at Asbury doesn't intersect your life in any way, you can pray for it or you can just never give it another thought—both perfectly valid responses under the circumstances."

I respectfully and deeply disagree.

My 86-year-old friend decided not to ignore what was happening. He did give it "another thought." The end of his note to me described how his continued search culminated in a wonderful personal reviving. His heart is so full that he said, "I am going to

---

[13] C.S. Lewis, "Mere Christianity," Harper, San Francisco, CA, 2001, Pg. 50

share this with our men's prayer group on Tuesday morning and my small group ... Maybe some of them have had the same problem. Thank you so much for helping me to be set free!"

When you encounter God and experience a new measure of His presence, you cannot help but tell others. It's the reviving, both personal and corporate, that we all need.

CHAPTER 13

EXTRAORDINARY PRAYER

MARCH 9, 2023

WHY SHOULD WE pray fervently for the blessing of a nationwide or worldwide spiritual awakening? Why should we unite (as Jonathan Edwards said) in "explicit agreement and visible union among God's people in extraordinary prayer for a revival of religion and the advancement of Christ's kingdom on earth?" Why should we seek to cooperate together and not tear apart the beginnings of His awakening in our nation?

Timothy Keller recently wrote an insightful article three days before the Asbury Awakening happened entitled, "American Christianity is Due for a Revival: Our society is secularizing, and Christianity seems to be in long-term decline. But renewal is possible." In that article, he speaks of the need for increased, united prayer.

> All religions promote and call for prayer. But historically, during times of fast growth and renewal, Christian movements have been marked by an extraordinary amount of communal prayer. During the early years of the explosive Christian movement in Korea, all-night prayer meetings were common, and they remain so in many parts of the country to this day. During the

18th-century Great Awakening in America, Jonathan Edwards wrote of the "explicit agreement and visible union of God's people in extraordinary prayer for the revival of religion." Unions of believers for prayer—both large and small gatherings—have an empowering effect. The renewed growth of the Church in the U.S. will not happen without it.[14]

Why should we increase our praying right now? Why should we pray with others, even momentarily laying aside some of our differences and joining together for a united cry for a nationwide awakening?

GOD'S BLESSINGS

The blessing of God is when He descends on something normal and makes it abnormal; natural and makes it supernatural; human and makes it Divine. For instance, when a boy gave five loaves and two fish, God blessed it and miraculously fed 5,000 people.

All of us pray for God's blessing. It's an oft-used phrase expressing our desire for God to take something to a dimension we could not see on our own. Think of the areas we pray for this blessing: "Lord bless our WORK ... our FAMILY ... our CHILDREN ... our CHURCH ... our NATION."

IT'S PERSONAL, BUT THERE'S MORE ...

Sometimes we pray for the blessings of God simply because we want them for ourselves. We desire the comfort, help, and pleasure

---

[14]Timothy Keller, *"American Christianity is Due for Revival,"* The Atlantic, February 5, 2023

they will bring. And the blessing of God provides all of this for us personally. But this is the *lowest level* of motivation to seek God's blessing. David, in Psalm 67, exhibits the *purest and highest level* of prayer.

> God be gracious to us and bless us, and cause His face to shine upon us—that Your way may be known on the earth, Your salvation among all nations.
>
> Let the peoples praise You, O God; let all the peoples praise You. Let the nations be glad and sing for joy; for You will judge the peoples with uprightness and guide the nations on the earth.
>
> Let the peoples praise You, O God; let all the peoples praise You. The earth has yielded its produce; God, our God, blesses us. God blesses us, that all the ends of the earth may fear Him. (Psalm 67:1-3, 7)

So, why should we seek the blessing of God in any area of our lives? And, in the highest way, why should we pray that God would bless our nation and world with an unusual outpouring of His presence and power ... a sweeping awakening that would bring our churches to life again and see the acceleration of the gospel?

The Psalmist instructs us in our praying. "Lord, bless us with your favor, presence, and power SO THAT...

YOUR WAY may be known on all the earth.

We should seek the hand and favor of God so that the ways in which He operates will be visible in every corner of the earth. One man said the church's task is to "give the world a right opinion of

God." The people around us see enough of the ways the world, flesh, and devil operate. They've even been turned away by how supposed Christians fight and argue (often about the most menial concerns). There are abundant illustrations of sinful paths and godless rebellion.

But a believer's life and a church's witness should show others the activity of the One whose "ways are higher than our ways and thoughts are higher than our thoughts" (Isaiah 55:8-9). Like the stunned crowd on the hillside, which had been miraculously fed from God's hand through a small boy's offering, God's manifest presence in times of spiritual awakening and the stunning results it produces bring into full view the reality that there is a better way than what mere man can produce.

YOUR SALVATION may extend among all nations.

When God showers visible blessing on His people, it is a witness unto the greatness of our God, which leads others to salvation. This may be in the form of provision for a need or grace amid suffering. But each blessing witnesses to others of a supernatural God.

"If I be lifted up," Jesus said, "I will draw all men unto Me" (John 12:32). This speaks not only of the manner of His death but the process that would one day bring people from every tongue and tribe and nation into His kingdom. When they see God working, it draws them to salvation. The reports of what God has done at Asbury have sped across the world at warp speed, and the result has been more people coming to Christ, many on college campuses and among the next generation. What could be more important?

Being saved from sin, death, and hell is the most important thing that can ever happen to any human. We should increase our prayers to this end and cry out for this salvation of people and nations so that...

YOUR PRAISE will come from all people.

God deserves honor and glory and praise. As men see His blessings and ways and are brought to salvation, more and more people will praise Him for His incredible goodness. They will worship and serve the Creator, who is blessed forever, and not the creature. *(see the opposite that we are experiencing in Romans 1:25)*

Seasons of intense revival and awakening across a region or nation bring God front and center. In His mercy, He makes Himself known. People see His ways and His nature. The result is the rapid expansion of the gospel and the growth of God's kingdom. We "see His salvation among the nations," which leads us to give God the praise He deserves.

John Piper said that "Missions exist because praise doesn't." The reason we must pray and ask God to make Himself known and aggressively cooperate with Him in explicit agreement, visible union, and extraordinary prayer is so that more people will bow before Him and give Him the glory He deserves.

We must pray—and pray fervently and unceasingly—for a mighty spiritual awakening for *His* sake.

CHAPTER 14

RESTORING THE HOUSE OF PRAYER

MARCH 10, 2023

IS PRAYER A nice thing to do? Something we resort to when we are in a serious situation? A word to describe one of the disciplines of the Christian life? Secondary, but not really all that essential? Something we do as a segue between songs on a Sunday morning?

Or is it the essence? The foundation? The fragrance that is to pervade everything for the serious follower of Jesus? The ultimate pathway to communion with God and the source of life and power for all we are and do?

A COMMUNITY MARKET

Jesus was in the last days of His life. As He passed through the temple mount area he was enraged that it had become a common market. A place designed by God for a sacred purpose had declined into merely a convenient, worldly merchandising hub with no thought of its glorious intent.

In His holy zeal, he wrecked the place, overturning tables and stopping traffic. And then He told them why. He reminded them of the sacred purpose of the temple environment.

My house shall be called a house of prayer for all the nations, but you have made it a robbers' den. (Mark 11:17)

THE TEMPLE

The temple was designed with Divine precision: an outer court, an inner room, and the Holy of Holies. Without describing the details, each section was created to bring a person deeper and deeper into the presence of God. The sacrifices in the outer areas were constantly burning for the sins of the people. (Imagine the incredible aroma as the sacrifices were burned, like a fine outdoor barbecue). It was filled with fragrances of repentance, humility, and cleansing. Of a recognition that we can only approach God through the sacrifice of the Messiah.

Outside the holy of holies was a room with a continual light burning, the "bread of the Presence," and the table on which incense burned incessantly. The innermost part of the temple represented the presence of God. It contained the Ark, which David had returned to Jerusalem. The Ark represented God's presence, from which everything flowed: His Word, His provision, His life.

What was the purpose of this place? It represented everything about how God and man connect. It was a place for Old Testament people to encounter God and commune with Him. To find the forgiveness needed and the relationship with the Father through His promised Son that covers and empowers everything. As we read the Bible, we find righteous people in Jesus' day continually going "up to the temple" for one purpose: to enter His presence through sacrificial faith, cleansing, and prayer.

Jesus was righteously angry when He saw that the temple was corrupted because this was His Father's house. It was sacred and holy. Its purposes were being ignored and prostituted. There were others places to house a market. This was to be a consecrated place where something Divine happened every moment of every day.

Prayer is a side experience for most of us today. But notice the single word that described all that should have been happening at the temple in Jesus' day (and ours): PRAYER. This was the word Jesus used about this place. This word summed up the essence of the temple and the essence of our relationship with God. Prayer is the pathway into His presence. A pathway in which we should live.

THE NEW TEMPLES

Our Bodies

In the New Covenant (New Testament) age, a shift occurred. Paul speaks of the temple in two ways: individually and corporately. He speaks of our bodies:

> *Or do you not know that your body is a temple of the Holy*
> *Spirit who is in you, whom you have from God, and that*
> *you are not your own? (1 Corinthians 6:19)*

The believer's physical body fulfills in one way what the temple in Jerusalem represented. We have three parts, just like the Jerusalem temple (body, soul, and spirit). And the great activity that once was done alone in the temple in Jerusalem has now shifted to us. We are to enter into His presence, through the sacrifice of Christ, and commune with God. We are to live in unceasing prayer. Our spirit is the place, eternally joined to His Spirit, in which the highest and holiest occurs. Prayer is the vehicle that allows us to consciously experience His presence.

How can we commune with Him and be used by Him if we are not in unceasing prayer? If the incense is not constantly rising from our lives, we have missed our purpose. This should represent a radical change in our thinking. Scripture-fed, Spirit-led prayer is not A thing, but THE thing. It is the vehicle by which our everyday lives fulfill the purposes of the temple—incense rising and our lives being consumed with the presence of God. This fragrance is to flow from our lives and draw others to Christ.

Our Churches

But Paul also speaks of our churches as a temple.

> Do you not know that you are a temple of God and that
> the Spirit of God dwells in you? (1 Corinthians 3:16)

Our gathering places for the Body of Christ can be many and varied. Around a tree in an African tribe, a humble church in a rural countryside, an elaborate building in a city, or a home in a persecuted country. We are scattered at times, but then we are called (and drawn by God) to gather.

But, if we are not careful, we can lose the intent of God about His church as we gather. The primary function of the gathered church is singular: like the Jerusalem temple, it is to be a place of prayer. This is why Jesus described it not as a place of community, or of preaching, or of worship, but of prayer. Both our bodies and our church gatherings should be filled with the fragrance of sacrifice and prayer. Our gatherings are the sacred spots where we encounter God corporately, continually, and deeply.

I have been in the gathered church when it is filled with the presence of God and the aroma of heaven. The loud noise of a lost world is outside, and our mission field is there. But among Christ's gathered Body, the sweet aroma of intentional prayer is everything. Our hearts are focused on the throne as everything flows from His presence. Rosalind Rinker said the great purpose of prayer is to make God the center of our attention and forget everything else. This should say much to us about what we do and the environments we create when we gather as one in the church.

UNCEASING PRAYER

"My house shall be called a house of prayer" came from both the lips of Isaiah and Jesus (Isaiah 65:7; Mark 11:17), reminding us of the primary importance of prayer. We are to pray without ceasing. We are to bring everything to God in prayer. Prayer is our means of connection with God and our source of abiding relationship and power. It is not a peripheral piece of true Christianity. Just as the temple held the highest place of prominence in Jerusalem and was the center of the city and of life, so our communion with God must be the same.

If prayer is a side room to us—both individually and collectively— we have missed the heart of the spiritual life. Notice that our greatest Christians were increasingly involved in elevating and illustrating prayer. They lived and moved in unceasing prayer, which was the source of their Christ-filled lives and effectiveness.

CLEANSING THE TEMPLE

What do we learn from Christ's zeal for His Father's house and His Father's purposes?

First, we must make our lives a house of prayer. When people encounter us, they should smell the incense and the sacrifices and encounter the presence of God. Our lives were made to experience God and to draw people to God. When people brush across our lives, they shouldn't notice the smell of the world, crowded with vendors calling for our attention, but the overwhelming fragrance of Christ. We should aggressively cooperate with God to make this a reality. And unceasing prayer is the means.

Secondly, the places we gather to worship Him corporately should be designed for communion with the Father. They should be filled with prayer. We should approach our gatherings just as a godly Jew would approach the temple in Jerusalem.

When did we stop praying? When did we begin to believe that we could build churches without talking with the Head? It is an undeniable and shameful fact that we have swallowed this lie, evidenced by the non-existence of prayer in most of our churches. This demonic thought cut us off from God's presence and power. We have elaborate wineskins, but little Wine. How did we get there, and what must we do to return to the unceasing lifestyle of prayer that exploded the early church?

There should be something about our gatherings of corporate worship that are atmospheric with the presence of God. I have been in places where to enter there is almost certainly to encounter Him. But sadly, I've also been in many gatherings where this is not the case. These churches are lifeless, void of His presence. We should think deeply about how to adjust our churches to make prayer the highway and His presence the destination.

As we enter, all of our attention should be upon Him (which is the essence of prayer). No worship team nor pastor should be our focus. They must be human leaders taking us into the Holy of Holies. The worship should lead us in. The testimonies of God's people should take us in (a lost element). Corporate prayer should take us in (another lost element). The Lord's Table should take us in.

The preaching should lead us in. The essence of all preaching should not be the brilliance of our exposition or oratory, but the glorious presence of Christ. This is not to degrade preaching, but to infuse it. The endgame of our proclamation should be a greater encounter with God's presence.

And, since God designed His church to be a house of prayer for ALL nations, any person from any background should be welcomed and overwhelmed there too. And all nations should be on our hearts and in our prayers just as they are with Christ.

And what would the result be if an unbeliever walked into our gatherings filled with His Presence?

> … he is convicted by all, he is called to account by all; the secrets of his heart are disclosed; and so he will fall on his face and worship God, declaring that God is certainly among you. (1 Corinthians 14:24-25)

And when a Presence-filled gathering occurs, we will leave those places and tell everyone about Jesus. We will find that we cannot help but speak about what we have seen and heard. Our witness will no more be a duty but an overflowing delight. We will want to bring everyone into an encounter with Him. Prayer does not keep us from the other vital functions of the church. It empowers and informs them.

A REVIVAL OF PRAYER

Asbury has informed us. And for the seeking hearts, it is reviving us, bringing us back.

If you entered Hughes auditorium at Asbury college during the sixteen glorious days in February 2023, you entered an incensed-laced room filled with Scripture-fed, Spirit-led, Worship-based prayer. Christ was at the center of it all. The oft-sung praise at Hughes was "You are worthy of it all." The veil was torn, and the room was alive with His presence. Nothing else mattered, and to be there was to encounter God.

This is why you could not leave. People who could only be there for an afternoon were frustrated that their time was limited, for heaven had come to Hughes. It was an approximation of the ultimate consummation (as David Bryant says). A taste of heaven because the people were being cleansed and communing with God. The roof was off, the walls were down, and the glory of God was covering the place like waters cover the sea.

And Christ turned over some tables to get us there. Schedules were interrupted, other priorities overturned. Time meant nothing. Money meant nothing. Food meant nothing. The pleasure of the world seemed ridiculous in light of His presence. Sins seemed foolish and were repented of gladly at the altar of prayer. The pull of the world was meaningless. People got on planes and came from overseas. Tables flipped over everywhere to make a highway so the King of glory could come in.

When the Lord gave a similar outpouring in the church I pastored in 2011 that led to five weeks of spontaneous gathering 3-4 hours a night, it was identical. The same fragrance and the same components were there. I have often said that this season at our church was a five-week continuous prayer meeting. We call it revival, and it was. It was God interrupting our schedules, waking us up from our spiritual lethargy and distracted Christianity, and bringing us back to where we should always live. He brought us back to unceasing prayer, allowing His presence to dominate everything. We saw more people spontaneously come to Christ in salvation than any other concentrated time. And we have never been the same.

AND NOW ...

How can we cooperate with God today to make our lives and churches houses of prayer? It is the singular description Christ used, and it should be the one description we use. It should be the passion of every believer and every church leader to make such a highway. As we look at Asbury and see the beauty of God's holiness in bold relief, we should not seek the exact particulars of Asbury but the purpose: to prepare a highway so God can manifest Himself and return His house to a house of prayer for all nations. To remove every boulder, both spiritually and structurally, that is an impediment on this highway.

Remember: Jesus is zealous about this. He will turn over tables to return His Father's places—individually and collectively—to their rightful purposes. He wants us in the temple with Him so that we will go to the nations with our faces aglow with His presence.

Father, may unceasing prayer make my life and the places I gather with other believers filled with Your fragrance and presence. And may we encounter You and help others encounter you in unceasing communion. Help us make any and every adjustment today to see that Your house is cleansed from the world, consumed with unceasing prayer, and alive with Your presence!

CHAPTER 15

WHAT DO YOU WANT?

MARCH 15, 2023

ALL OF US are drawn like a magnet to what we think will give us satisfaction. Some of these attractions are overtly sinful (moral impurity, for instance), while others seem mindless and seemingly harmless. But, when anything is a substitute for God, it becomes deadly to the spiritual life. The smallest misdirection can become a disastrous detour from God. It's not the road you take, but the road you miss. Satan knows this, and his arsenal is filled with detour signs.

A SOLITARY DESIRE

The Psalmist had been momentarily confused (Psalm 73). Worldly men looked like they had the best. His religious life seemed tedious and unfruitful.

But he experienced a glorious revival. He "came into the sanctuary," and was pulled back into clarity. He saw that a godless man's end is disastrous. And suddenly for the Psalmist, all the world's alluring treasures paled in comparison to God Himself.

Whom have I in heaven but You? And besides You, I desire nothing on earth. My flesh and my heart may fail, but God

is the strength of my heart and my portion forever. For,
behold, those who are far from You will perish; You have
destroyed all those who are unfaithful to You. But as for
me, the nearness of God is my good. I have made the Lord
GOD my refuge, that I may tell of all Your works. (Psalm
73:25-28)

But look deeply into the Psalmist's heart. He speaks of the experiential. Not only did he believe in God. He longed for and experienced the "nearness" of God. He was delighting in genuine intimacy with God. He found what he longed for, not in knowing about God, but knowing God.

A CHOICE

This nearness did not happen accidentally. *"I have made the Lord God my refuge,"* the Psalmist said. It was a choice. Countless gods called for his allegiance, but he had seen the beauty of the Lord in the sanctuary and had deliberately chosen Him. Like Mary, who sat at the Lord's feet and chose "the good part that will not be taken away from her," the Psalmist had turned his affections in one direction. Both Mary and Martha were around Jesus (a good place to be). Martha was distracted, but Mary was changed because of her deliberate choice to pursue the Presence.

James, the brother of Jesus, lays this responsibility squarely on our shoulders also. "Draw near to God, and He will draw near to you" (James 4:8). God promises intimacy, but this promise is contingent upon our approach.

This is the heart of revival, both personal and corporate. Revival indicates two things have occurred: a drifting and a return. We have wandered from Christ. Our hearts have become cold and lifeless. To be revived is to be brought back to that which is life itself. It's not a return to a program or a discipline alone. It is to fall in love with Jesus all over again. It is a repentance unto Him.

I spoke to a pastor today who is faithful and capable. He's been doing a good job at his church. But in the last two weeks, hearing of God's outpouring at Asbury, he has sought the Lord and God has met him in great measure. He cannot believe the difference. He told me that everything is changing in his life, his marriage, and his work. He tried to explain the glory of God's presence in his truck during a two-hour drive this morning and his eyes filled with tears and he could not speak.

He told me that last week, there was an area of sin that he indulged in, and the Spirit prompted him to confess it and repent. But he refused, thinking it was insignificant. The next day, God's presence seemed nowhere to be found until he resolved the matter. He could not bear the thought of living anymore without the conscious awareness of God's presence. He is drawing near, and so is His gracious Father.

THE ALL OF GOD

My brother, Tom, once captured this truth in a sentence.

> *"If a man can ever come to the place in his life where all he wants is all God wants, then all his life he'll have all he wants, and God will have all He wants of him."*

The man who has come to this place is richer than any billionaire, for all his life he will have Christ. He doesn't need the world's goods, for God is his portion. Like Paul, he "has nothing yet possesses all things."

God doesn't just give this man strength; He IS his strength. His protection is secure, for God is his refuge. His purpose will be delightful, for he has returned to that for which he was created and delights in the joy of telling others of all God's works. Stars were created for the sky and fish for the sea. Man was made to experience and glorify God, and we find our purpose nowhere else.

In the glorious seasons when God sends corporate revival to His people, (as He has done at Asbury and is doing in some measure across the nation,) why do you see people bowing low in worship and standing with arms raised in glorious praise? Why the awe? Why the unashamed testimonies? In His grace, God has revealed Himself, and needy seekers have dropped the world's substitutes at the altar and run to the One who alone delights them.

But we must not be spectators. Have you been distracted? Drawn away from the simplicity and purity of devotion to Christ alone? Then run into the sanctuary with the Psalmist. Join the revived. Seek Christ and you will find Him. And in the finding, you will have all you want, and He will have all He wants of you.

CHAPTER 16

HE IS WORTHY OF IT ALL

MARCH 24, 2023

IN THE RECENT outpouring at Asbury University, there was one song that filled the room over and over again, sometimes for hours. It has been one month since the night and day services at Asbury ended (although the reviving work of God continues and expands), but this song is so embedded that many of us who attended find ourselves singing it throughout the day. It expresses what's in our hearts. To sing it is to step back into the place of His manifest presence.

> *You are worthy of it all.*
> *You are worthy of it all.*
> *For from You are all things,*
> *And to You are all things.*
> *You deserve the glory.*
> *Day and night, night and day let incense arise!*[15]

This song comes from Paul's beautiful benediction in Romans 11. It is characteristic of Paul that he often comes to a point in his Spirit-breathed writing that he can go no further without erupting

---

[15]Written by Phil Wickham, Ryan Hall, and David Brymer; April 8, 2022

in worship. A glorious benediction flows from his heart as he is overwhelmed with God.

> *Oh, the depth of the riches, both of the wisdom and knowl-edge of God! How unsearchable are His judgments and unfathomable His ways! For who has known the mind of the Lord, or who became His counselor? Or who has first given to Him that it might be paid back to him again?* **For from Him and through Him and to Him are all things. To Him be the glory forever. Amen.** *(Romans 11:33-36)*

Words like this erupt from those who have seen God, who have been overwhelmed by a fresh understanding of the Almighty. The proud man never sings these words. A self-absorbed man lifts a song of himself, which is a tragic, myopic tune based on the big lie that the creature is more important than the Creator. It is like an ant being so blinded by arrogance that he doesn't even notice the man who towers above him.

"Blessed are the pure in heart," Jesus said, "For they will see God." And this purity comes by recognizing our spiritual poverty with such depth that we mourn and then, in brokenness, bow be-fore the Lord in glad submission (see this foundational progression in Matthew 5:3-8). When we are purged from a self-consumed life, we begin to see that everything is from God, through God, and to God.

RADICAL HUMILITY

This is why the wise leaders during the blessed days of revival at Asbury continued to remind us that we must walk in radical humility. The more we let Christ fill our gaze, the less we think of ourselves. We find, as Timothy Keller says, "the freedom of self-forgetfulness." This is the posture of the revived.

Revival restores God to His rightful place in our hearts, our minds, and our lives. God magnified. God worshiped. God adored. God loved. God served. God boldly shared with everyone around us. And when He fills our vision, everything is returned to its rightful place.

God is making Himself known during these days, not just at Asbury. I was with 30 revival leaders this week and heard the testimony of three pastors who, combined, have seen hundreds of conversions in the last two months. Also, from two leaders from Indonesia and India where revival winds are blowing. From both leaders and students at Baylor University where 2,000 students gathered for 72 hours to seek God this week.

In multiple churches where I've had the privilege to speak the altars have been full in every service, and I've heard this testimony from many pastors. There is an unusual expectancy and extraordinary prayer continuing. Aslan is on the move.

You can ignore this or explain it away, but if you seek Him, you will find Him. Do not seek revival ... seek Him. And as you do, He will put a new song on your lips that you cannot stop singing.

LEADING TIMES OF TESTIMONY

Historically, one of the primary ingredients for the spread of revivals has been personal testimonies. The accounting of the work of God in individual hearts can prove a powerful tool in the hands of God to inspire, encourage, and convict others.

Often pastors are fearful of public testimony times for the following reasons:

- embarrassingly "dry" testimonies

- excessive long or emotional testimonies

- testimonies that step over lines of propriety

- non-specific, generalized testimonies that appear useless and unedifying

- Immature or attention seeking people monopolizing time at the microphone

Testimonies can provide freedom for God to accomplish considerable good in the following ways:

- Give God the glory due Him as He transforms lives.

- Help believers confirm and verbalize what God is doing in their lives.

- Allow specific testimonies to inspire, convict, encourage, teach, and train other believers.

- Grow the church through a fresh sense of the magnitude of God's work in their church.

- Give the pastor an opportunity to identify and "preach" on certain themes that are repeatedly mentioned during testimonies.

- Provide a spiritual "thermometer" by giving church leaders an increased understanding of where God is at work and by identifying primary areas of need.

- Give opportunity for public confession and corporate forgiveness.

The following are hints on how to lead an effective testimony time. The average lay person may be as fearful regarding these times as a pastor, often because of bad experiences in the past. Carefully explaining how the sharing time will be conducted can pave the way for a fresh release of God's Spirit through His people in the body.

Pray! Spend time privately and publicly praying for:

- God to bring the right people to share.

- protection from the enemy.

- wisdom, as the pastor, to know how to lead the time—particularly how to be sensitive to key points of conviction.

Take time to educate the congregation on how to give a testimony. The following model might be used.

1. Share how each person has a unique spiritual pilgrimage that can encourage others. Learning to articulate and transparently communicate God's activity in your life is one of the great keys to usefulness for God's kingdom.

2. Describe how to share a testimony.

   - Share where God found you. Be specific regarding areas of sin and need.

   - Share what you were experiencing as a result of controlling your own life.

   - Share what God said to you.

   - Share how you responded. You may have responded negatively at first . . . be honest.

   - Share what you are now experiencing as a result of obedience to God's truth. What benefits of obedience are you experiencing?

3. Describe simple ground rules.

   - Be brief.

   - Be specific.

   - Be current.

   - Bring all the glory to God.

- Don't reflect negatively on others.
- Use the term "moral failure" for any moral sins.

4. Invite the congregation to think of one area where God has been working in recent days (you may want to identify this as the past week, month, six months, etc.). Then ask members to turn to one other person and, using the above method, share a three-minute testimony.

5. Spend a moment in prayer. Let members ask God whether He wants them to share a public testimony. Invite those who feel led to share to come and be seated on the front row. Indicate that you may or may not get to all those who came forward. This gives the pastor the discretion to choose those he feels led to call upon.

6. As they come, the pastor can stand by the microphone with those who are sharing. Feel free to interrupt and help them clarify or give further specifics if needed. Offer encouragement and love. At times you may have to shut down a testimony that is entirely off track or disruptive to what God is doing. Make sure you always keep control of the microphone!

7. Lead in ministering to people after they have shared.

- Give a word of encouragement or affirmation, if appropriate.
- If they have asked for the church's forgiveness, lead the church in corporately verbalizing forgiveness to the individual.

- Invite people to give a hug or a word of encouragement to those testifying as they head back to their seats.

- If the testifier still has needs or burdens, invite a group of concerned people to gather around that person or take them to a side room for prayer, encouragement, counsel, or other needed help.

8. Be sensitive not only to the person testifying, but to what God is saying to the church through the testimony. Remind the people that they are not spectators but participants. God may be speaking directly to them about related issues. When a similar testimony is repeated several times, recognize this as God speaking to the church.

9. Be sensitive to opportunities to exhort or preach based on the testimonies. Don't feel the need to speak after every testimony. If God brings to your mind key thoughts that help crystallize and convict through the testimonies, seize the opportunity, perhaps even stopping to give people an opportunity to respond to what has just been said.

Other helpful hints include:

1. Don't worry about excesses. If someone seems to step over the line in some way, discreetly take control of the microphone and thank God publicly that people feel the freedom to share, then gently remind folks of the boundaries for the testimonies.

2. When people share things that should have been related in private, ask them to go to that individual immediately, if possible, to clear their conscience.

3. Don't feel you must have everyone share publicly. It is often better to stop on a significant note instead of dragging it out. If you extend the sharing time too long, some people may feel they need to say something even though God has not been doing a special work in their life. This will also leave the congregation anxious to hear more from God the next time they meet. Inform those who did not get to share that there will be other opportunities and affirm that they have been obedient to God by being willing to share.

4. Remind people that every testimony is significant.

Although the above suggestions may seem mechanical, they have proven helpful to many. Trust God to use you to open the way of blessing to others through this wonderful and biblical practice. "Let the redeemed of the Lord say so" (Psalm 107:2).[16]

[16] Bill Elliff, appendix in *Fresh Encounter: God's Pattern for Spiritual Awakening* by Henry Blackaby, Richard Blackaby, and Claude King (Nashville: B&H Publishing Group, 2009) 294-297. Reprinted and used by permission.

Additional copies and other resources can be found at

`http://www.billelliff.com`

Made in the USA
Columbia, SC
16 April 2023

15086847R00083